Never Far From Home

Never Far From Home

The story of my life

JOHN KNOX

1900

WORD BOOKS
Waco, Texas

Never Far From Home

Library of Congress catalog card number: 74–82657
Printed in the United States of America

**For
my two sons
Jack and Tony**

Contents

Foreword 9

1. Memories of Boyhood 11

2. Life at School 29

3. Doubts and Searchings 45

4. At Fisk University 62

5. Some Disappointed Hopes 82

6. Chicago: 1934–1943 97

7. The Years at Union: 1943–1966 116

8. Our Life in Austin: 1965–1972 148

Foreword

Some months ago I decided to use part of my retirement leisure in writing a brief story of my life, making it as accurate
and consecutive as memory would permit, for I have kept no
diary or other records. I intended the sketch simply as a gift
to my sons, realizing how much such an account of my own
father's life would mean to me if I possessed it. What I wrote
was in the form of a letter, and I began and completed it
with no thought of its being read except by my sons, to whom
it was addressed, and perhaps by a very few others. But an
old friend, after inquiring what I had been doing, kindly suggested that the "letter" might be interesting to a wider circle
of readers. When another friend, having actually read the
piece, expressed the same opinion, I was bold enough to sub-
mit it to the present publisher; and he was bolder still—
he accepted it! With some changes in format, it is here presented.

Because the narrative was originally addressed to members
of my family, less is said *about* them than would have been
the case if I had been consciously writing for publication.
And because it was my intention from the beginning to be
brief and summary, I do not mention even by name most of
the friends I have loved along the way. I regret both omissions but see no way at this stage of repairing them.

9

I suspect that many authors and publishers of memoirs, long and short, have trouble settling on appropriate titles. More often than not perhaps the chosen titles suggest the movement and change of a journey. In my own case there has surely been enough of change and movement to justify such a title. (I note that I have just now used the phrase "along the way.") But despite all the changes, in the world and in myself, my dominant impression, as I look back on my life, is that I have never been far from home. What I mean by that statement and why I find it true, I hope the following pages will reveal.

JOHN KNOX

Medford Leas
Medford, N.J.
August, 1974

Chapter 1

Memories of Boyhood

MY EARLIEST REMEMBRANCE is distinct and vivid; it has no vague background in the half-remembered as, I gather, first memories often do. It is of my arrival by train at Confluence, in western Pennsylvania, with our family—my father and mother, Absalom and Emma Mann Knox, and my two sisters, Virginia and Eva. Eva was a baby; Virginia would have been three or four years old; and I, five or six. I saw—and this would have been my very first remembered image—through the soiled window of the railway coach the man and woman who, I soon discovered, were there to meet us and whose names proved to be Mr. and Mrs. Liston. I recall only vaguely the moment of greeting and introduction, but more clear are moments in our ride of ten miles or so in their surrey, to Listonburg, which was to be our home for the next two years.

To me this arrival seemed marvelously important—we were to live in a new home in a new land. But to my parents it had an importance far more real and poignant, of which I could not have dreamed. For them it meant nothing less than the beginning of a whole new life.

From a time before my birth or even their marriage in 1900, my father had been a YMCA secretary. He had served in that capacity, not only in several southern cities, but also, for the brief duration of the Spanish-American War, as an enlisted volunteer soldier assigned by the army to this special service. The YMCA in those days, and indeed through the time of my youth, was an institution very different in kind from the largely secular institution it has now become. It was then primarily an arm of the church, a Christian organization, rendering various social services, but most actively concerned with exercising an evangelical and pastoral function among young men. My father, denied by the poverty of his family any formal education beyond the grades, if in fact as far as that, had spent the greater part of his boyhood and early youth as a worker on his father's poor post-Civil War farm in Mississippi and later as a salesman in his uncle's store in Pine Bluff, Arkansas. But soon after he was twenty, under the influence of the YMCA, he felt a call to service in that organization. He entered the Chicago YMCA College, attending school by day and supporting himself with a night job in a small short-order restaurant (thus, my mother always thought, permanently undermining his health). After graduation from the two-year training course, he went to Paducah, Kentucky, for his first secretary's job, and seven or eight years later was holding the corresponding position in the YMCA of Roanoke, Virginia.

But now came a crisis in his inner life—the conviction that his real calling was that of a minister. I can only imagine the agonizing conversations which must have taken place between him and my mother as they considered the radical changes and the considerable sacrifices which would be involved if they made a positive response. But the final decision was inevitable. He was eventually admitted to the Baltimore Conference of the old Southern Methodist Church (now included in a larger whole), and was assigned to its northernmost, and from every worldly point of view its least attractive, parish. And thus I return to the point where my remembered life begins, the very end of what must have been the long and arduous trip of our family of five from Roanoke to Listonburg.

Listonburg, as I remember it, was a village of a few scattered frame houses strung along a large creek and completely dominated by a coal mine—whether great or small as coal mines go, I have no idea. For us it was simply "the mine." Although it was within sight of our house, it seemed a long way off, and I do not believe I ever actually visited it; certainly I have no recollection of doing so. The Listons lived in the village's "big house," separated from the parsonage, with its small front and back yards, by what seems in my mind to have been an exceedingly broad meadow. I do not remember our barn and outhouse or privy, but they were surely there, deep in the backyard. A dirt road ran along the fronts of both houses and, beyond the road by only a few feet, "the creek." The post office and general store were farther along the creek beyond the Listons' house. I have the vaguest kind of memory of them and no memory at all of a school—which is not surprising since all of us were too young to attend one. The church I do recall as being a white wooden one-room structure looking down on our house from higher ground across the creek.

My father's parish contained six churches, all of them smaller and even more rural than the Listonburg church itself, and much of his time needed to be spent on the road. Not only were there preaching services in each church in alternate weeks, three each Sunday, but constant visits during the weeks to persons in need of pastoral help, not to mention such occasions as marriages and funerals in various parts of the parish area. He traveled usually by buggy and horse, and I often accompanied him. Even in winter, when the deep snow made buggy travel impossible, he often took me with him horseback, and I would ride behind him in the saddle.

I cannot recall any of these many trips in particular, but in a general way I recall them very vividly—and very gratefully. They were for me at the time great adventures, and, more important as I think of them in retrospect, they offered the best opportunities I had for intercourse with my father. These long rides, whether by buggy or on horseback, along the quiet mountain roads gave almost unlimited opportunity for talk, as well as for the silence which, when it falls between persons who love each other, can often be more full of shared meaning than any speech. Almost as important in this intercourse was the privilege thus provided me of hearing my father preach, not seldom the same sermon two or three times to the different congregations he would meet on a single Sunday.

I have been speaking of the time in Listonburg. But the same kind of association, with very few interruptions, continued. Two years later at Strasburg in the Shenandoah Valley of Virginia he had a similar assignment, several rural churches scattered over a beautiful, though less rugged, terrain. A little later at Stephens City, Virginia, and later still at Shepherdstown, West Virginia, both some miles north of Strasburg in the same valley, his situation was essentially the same. Indeed, through all this early period, into my high school years, the trips with my father, as he visited his churches or their members, stand out in my memory, and no other kind of experience belonging to my boyhood do I remember with greater pleasure or think of with deeper gratitude.

Father's salary at Listonburg was $600 a year. The use of the parsonage was an important perquisite; but even so, since neither he nor my mother had any independent income, we were anything but rich. When we moved to Strasburg, the salary rose to $800. It was only in the last four or five years of his brief life—he died at fifty, just eighteen

years after the scene at Confluence I have described—that
our family income rose above the $2000 mark. It hardly needs
to be said that we were, throughout my boyhood, poor according to any definition of the term. Only much later could I
have realized the economies my parents must have practiced
all those years. And yet we were never in debt, and I do not
recall feeling any special deprivation. My mother must have
felt the stringency very acutely, although I was never made
aware of this by any complaint, whether in word or manner.

During at least two periods of some length very early in
my remembered life, the demands made on her by two or
three small children, when added to the regular, and enormous, burdens of housekeeping in those days, required that
we have a servant. My father was a good housekeeper and
a really excellent cook, but there were times when he could
not give her the necessary relief. I remember only two of
these helpers, Sally and Annie, and perhaps there were no
others. These servants lived in, quite as members of the
family, and we all became very fond of them. How my father
was able to afford this necessary luxury, I do not understand.
Surely, the wages must have consisted almost entirely in the
lodging and food provided.

I have said that my mother must have found our poverty
an especially grievous burden. This can be surmised, not only
because so much of the weight of poverty always falls most
directly on the wife and mother, but also because my mother
would have lacked, naturally and inevitably, the same sense
of vocation and the same satisfaction in fulfilling it which
would have made any material sacrifice acceptable to my
father so long as it affected only himself. That this sacrifice
did *not* affect only himself he was acutely aware. During
those years, and indeed till the end of his life, he often spoke
to me of his grief that he could not provide better for his
family's needs.

He felt this, I know, the more keenly because my mother's

circumstances before her marriage had been fairly comfortable. Poverty was prevalent in the South just after the War between the States, and it would not be true to say that my mother's family escaped—far from it! Still, she had been in this respect more fortunate than my father. She had been brought up in some comfort and had enjoyed a good education, graduating from what is now Lambuth College in Jackson, near her Brownsville, Tennessee, home. The family soon afterward moved to Pine Bluff, Arkansas, and my mother became a very successful and a much loved teacher in the public schools of that city. Her family was a large one; she had eight sisters, all but three older than she, and three older brothers. All but one of her sisters had married, and the husbands were successful business or professional men. Her three brothers, even as early as the time of her marriage, were embarked on prosperous careers and were providing abundantly for their mother, our grandmother, and the one unmarried sister, who cared for her. My sisters and I thought of all this large tribe (many of them, especially our grandmother, known and very dear to us) as Croesuses or Midases and spoke of them with a kind of awe. Needless to say, we exaggerated their wealth, but it was still quite true that my mother was the one member of this large and very intimate family who was not relatively affluent. She could hardly have helped feeling this discrepancy, and undoubtedly my father felt it very deeply.

But unless I am careful, I shall convey the impression that we were an unhappy family. Nothing could be farther from the truth. We children, though we were poor, were not aware of being so. My father was sustained by his clear assurance that he was doing the work God intended him to do, in which he found great joy, and in which alone he could have been even content. And my mother, despite all I have said, was one of the most cheerful persons I have ever known. She had a delightful and never-failing sense of humor, as did my father also—and they needed it! Although later—after my boyhood years—I realized that she was especially subject to anxieties of various kinds, still she had the good humor, the natural buoyancy, the strength and courage, and, one might add, the obstinacy, necessary to transcend them and to be happy in spite of them. Her husband and children were a preoccupation in which she took both joy and pride. She was a warm and loving person, of keen intelligence and lively wit, attracting and holding friends, wherever we lived. As far as her health and her cares for her children and home would permit, she entered cheerfully and creatively into my father's work.

I have spoken of my father's earliest life as the son of a poor farmer in Mississippi and mentioned especially his lack of schooling. But this must not be taken to mean that he was an uneducated, much less an uncultivated, man. His mother had died when he was very young, and I do not recall his often speaking of her, though I knew he could remember her and that he thought of her with reverence and love. She was, I gathered, a lady of a rather wealthy family (before the War), and of superior personal gifts. The widower married again, at least early enough for the new wife to have had a significant part in the rearing of my father and his sister and four brothers. It was always my impression, however, that it was his father who had exercised the predominant influence in my own father's early years. He had died before I was born; but I have a clearer image of him than of either his mother or his stepmother, not only because my father often spoke of him, but also because I have several letters of his to "Absie," as my father was known to all his old friends and relatives—except to my mother who, after the strange fashion of the times, never referred to him but as "your father" or "Mr. Knox," and who never addressed him, at least in my hearing, in any other than the latter way.

My grandfather was the great, great grandson of a John Knox who had emigrated to this country from Scotland, by way of Ireland, before the middle of the eighteenth century and had settled in North Carolina. All but the eldest of his several sons had, one by one, moved westward, and my own ancestor had found his place in Mississippi. I know little of the early life of my father's father. I do know that he was a college graduate, that he entered army service at the beginning of the War between the States, and that at its end he had attained the rank of captain, having served for a time, as I remember, in the forces of General Nathan Forrest. I know also that in the post-bellum period he was for a while a member of the Mississippi legislature. His letters, as well as the remembered remarks of my father, reveal him as a man of integrity, intelligence, and humane feeling, deeply concerned about, and warmly devoted to, his family. My father evidently responded to his tender regard with respect, loyalty and affection.

No one brought up in such a home, however little schooling he may have, can be "uneducated," even if one has only average intellectual capacities and moral and aesthetic sensitivities. But my father was far above average in all of these respects. He had read, and habitually read, good books. In the period when I knew him, these were, for the greater part, religious or theological books—books directly pertinent to his dominant interest and to his work. But his liking for literature was not thus limited. I recall especially his love of Dickens, whose novels he read over and over again. *Pickwick Papers* was his almost constant bedside companion. He spoke well, whether in public or in private conversation. His sermons— in the beginning one every two weeks and, in his later years when he served a single church with both morning and evening services, two every week—were always carefully prepared and fully written out, although he never referred to a manuscript or even to notes in his actual preaching. He had extraordinary gifts as a storyteller and a prodigious memory for anecdotes, particularly of a humorous sort, and was in great demand as an after-dinner speaker—not that Liston-burg or any of his early rural parishes offered many occasions of this kind!

Knowing how little schooling he had had, and this probably of an inferior quality, I have often wondered at the distinguished character of my father's writing—for it *was* distinguished. Where or how did he learn to write so well, not only with coherency and clarity, but also with "style"? Perhaps, he gained this competency from his reading. Perhaps, if such things can be, it was a native gift. I know it was not simply the result of sermon-writing, for I have the letter in which he asked my mother's mother for her daughter's hand, and it possesses the same simplicity and charm which all his later writing exemplified. Possibly, he wrote well, not because he had learned much, but rather because he had so little to "unlearn." He was himself simple and charming and had only to write as he thought and felt.

I remember well the time when, in the sixth or seventh grade of school, I was given my first assignment of a composition. I felt hopelessly lost as I faced the task and spoke to him of my perplexity about both subject and manner of treatment. He suggested a subject which lay plainly within my experience and indicated several natural ways in which it might be approached and developed. I saw at once what he meant and never had to appeal to him in such a connection again. The most important lesson I ever had in the art of writing—a more important lesson, I should say, than all the later formal lessons combined—was this conversation with my unschooled father. I have spent most of my life in educational work, but if ever I am tempted to think too highly of its importance, to assess anyone's competence simply by the amount of it he has had, to place much value on academic degrees merely as such, I think of my father and know infallibly how false such judgments are.

For his pastoral work he was superbly gifted—devoted, patient, compassionate, tactful, eager and able to understand, wise, and above all perhaps, gentle. I believe it is strictly true to say that there was no one who knew my father who did not both respect and love him.

I have spoken of my mother's physical strength as hardly equal to her heavy load of duties in home and parish. She was, when I first remember her, a rather slender person of average height, with blue eyes and blonde hair and with a strikingly lively expression except at times of occasional illness or of unusual strain and fatigue. These times were distressing to us all, especially, needless to say, to her and my father. Her strength increased in proportion to the lessening of her cares as we children grew older, and during her later years her health was quite good. My father, however, as I have already hinted, was never physically strong, and only great self-discipline and constant attention to diet prevented his being often ill. He was very slight in build; only after I myself was grown did I realize how very small a man he was. I do not recall the measure of his height, but I suspect that it could not have been more than seven or eight inches above five feet; I do remember that his normal weight was 115 pounds. As to facial features, I shall say only that he had blue eyes and light brown hair and that his appearance, as my mother's also, suited the characters I have tried to describe. Both of them appeared to be entirely what they were—intelligent, sensitive, cheerful and loving persons.

I do not want to give the impression that our family life was lived in a paradise or that in our early years we children (soon after our moving to Strasburg a fourth, our brother James, was born) somehow missed the heartache and the thousand natural shocks. Nor would I wish it to appear that I thought our parents perfect people or perfect parents— although I confess I cannot imagine better ones. Neither of them was a placid, complacent person—not that such a disposition would have been a virtue! Both were capable of swift and sometimes uncalled for anger. My father more than once said in my hearing that he felt his besetting sin was impatience, and he meant undoubtedly impatience with the recalcitrances and impetuosities of his children. I have spoken of the "obstinacy" of my mother, regarding it as an element in her ability to bear with some serenity and joy the often bitter burdens her circumstances imposed. But, needless to say, this obstinacy had also its less positive side.

She was an extraordinarily firm and resolute person, especially when she thought the welfare of her children was concerned. I recall the Saturday night in Shepherdstown at the end of my first week on a summer job as delivery boy at the local hardware store. I reached home about nine o'clock to discover that I had lost the six dollars just paid me for my week's work. I went to bed almost in tears. But at breakfast next morning I found my six dollars by my plate. Having inquired the preceding evening what route I had followed on my way home, my mother had risen long before day and, retracing my steps, had found the money near the door of a house where I had left a parcel en route. She was not easily defeated!

But, as I have hinted, this character could manifest itself less admirably and productively. Occasionally at least it led to strain between her and her children and also, no doubt, between her and my father, although I do not have any actual evidence of this. Once having taken a position—and she may have taken it impulsively—she found it hard to change it.

I remember well an incident in my own experience which illustrates this trait of my mother. I had done something wrong in school and had concealed it from my teacher—I do not remember just what the wrong deed was. After I had come home, my troubled conscience permitted me no rest till I had written my teacher and confessed my fault. A day or so later I received a most kind and forgiving note from her. My mother saw the envelope, knew that it came from my teacher, and asked to see the note. I indicated my unwillingness to share it, saying that it concerned a private matter and that everything had been satisfactorily settled. But my mother insisted so strongly and persistently that I was finally forced to put the note into her hands. One of the most vivid memories of my childhood is the look of shame on her face when she returned it. But she said nothing; she was unwilling, or unable, to acknowledge her fault in words. It means no virtue in me but is a sign of the mores in parent-child relations of the time, as well of the general or habitual relationship of understanding and love between my mother and me, that I felt no resentment. I understood her look as an apology, and it would not have occurred to me to doubt her authority. I tell this little story as an example of the strength and obstinate devotion of my mother, which had its good and its unfortunate sides. She would have defended her children literally to the death from any outside danger or attack, but she did not always see that this very devotion might itself be threatening or hurtful.

My father, though he loved us quite as much and was almost as much with us, was less subject to this fault. No loving parent, I dare say, is able to escape it altogether; and I would not claim so much as that for him, but he was more discerning and sensitive than my mother in this regard. I feel sure that, for all the interest he would have felt, he would not have asked to see the teacher's note, and it would have been quite impossible for him to *insist* on seeing it. Another incident illustrates my father's attitude.

There was a period in my boyhood when I was addicted to the reading of the books of Horatio Alger. My sisters, too, came to share this interest to a degree. One Christmas, I recall, I spent my small allowance on a number of these books as presents for them with the idea that I should be able to read them also. This happened only once, but it was a long time before I heard the end of it! My mother made great fun of the stories. I remember her entertaining us, at a time when we were all down with mumps or measles and gathered in a single room, by reading them to us, accentuating by improvised insertions of her own the absurdities of the tales. This must have occurred at a time when the stories had begun to lose their appeal. In any case, we were greatly amused.

But earlier the Alger stories had been far from a laughing matter; at any rate, this was true for me. My father was a little impatient with my preoccupation with these cheap books, but made no strong objection. Having rather strict views about proper Sunday observance, however, he did ask that I not read them on that day. I shall not forget the moment when he found me one Sunday afternoon sitting in half darkness on an unused stairway in our Stephens City house reading an Alger story. I was overcome with embarrassment and shame. Mercifully he seemed to pay no attention at the time. But a little later he made an occasion for speaking to me. He told me that although he had hoped I might be willing on Sundays to give up Alger books for more serious occupations, still it was far more important to be honest and open than to keep even the most important regulation about Sunday, or any similar observance. If my own conscience permitted the reading and I so much wished to do it, he wanted me to continue it, whatever the day, without any attempt at concealment. Such wisdom about relative values which this incident reveals was one of my father's most remarkable characteristics.

It goes without saying that this description of our family's life in my boyhood years is only the briefest possible sketch. No doubt, it will to some extent be filled in by references to these years as we proceed, although I cannot hope to make the account full and clear or to put into words what stand only as vivid pictures in my memory. But even a brief sketch would be woefully inadequate if something more were not said about the most important reality in our family's situation and experience—namely, the church and its life.

I have spoken of the religious sensitivities of my father and of the early Christian commitment which issued finally in his decision to enter the professional ministry. Perhaps I should not use that phrase, for there was certainly nothing merely professional in my father's vocation. The ministry was his only authentic way of being himself, as every profession ought to be perhaps and as the profession of a minister *must* be if it is to have any worth or true success at all. I do not recall his ever speaking of any crisis in his early experience which might be called a conversion, and therefore am doubtful that such a crisis occurred, although I cannot rule it out. His mother, I gathered, had been a very sensitive and religiously devout woman; and although she died when he was no more than four years old, her influence had been important, perhaps even decisive. His father, I know, for all my own father's debt to him and loyalty toward him, had been only conventionally Christian, if indeed he professed to be a Christian at all. But however it came about, my father was a deeply religious man. And although obviously it would not necessarily have followed from that fact that he should enter the ministry, it is not at all surprising that he did. His religious vocation was of a piece with his whole life as a man.

His mother had been a Methodist, and he had always been a member of that denomination, though the Knox family connection had been and is predominantly Presbyterian. He became a Methodist minister, and I have already said enough about his first appointment and our move to Listonburg.

The word *appointment* may sound strange in some ears, for in this connection it is almost a technical term. I have not been in active connection with the Methodist Church for the last forty years and cannot speak of the current state of things within that church as regards the location of clergy. But at the time of which I am speaking and in our part of the church, ministers in a particular area belonged to a "conference," over several of which a bishop, designated to do so periodically by a council of bishops, presided. It was the duty of this bishop and lay strictly within his power to appoint annually every minister in each conference to the parish within its bounds which he was to serve during the ensuing year. Occasionally, a minister could be appointed to a church in another conference, but in such a case his own consent was required. The bishop was supposed to take counsel from the presiding elders, also appointed by him as superintendents of churches within the smaller units, or districts, into which the conference was divided for administrative purposes; but the prerogative of appointment belonged finally and solely to him. Changes in appointment for any particular minister came rather often. The average length of a minister's stay in a parish was, I should say, from two to three years, and in no case could he remain longer than four years in one place.

Since so much of a vitally practical kind depended on its outcome, it is not surprising that the big event of the year, not merely for the minister but for his family quite as much, was the annual meeting of the conference. And the big

event of the conference—for the minister's family the only
event worth mentioning—was the bishop's reading of the ap-
pointments, which was always the final happening of the
week-long session. My father not infrequently took me with
him on these annual trips to one of the cities within the
conference's bounds, to Washington, or Baltimore, or Cum-
berland, or Roanoke, or some other city able to accommodate
so large a meeting of clergy and lay delegates. And more
than a few times I knew the excitement of sitting in a church
building as one of a large congregation where some two or
three hundred ministers, most of them with families, hung
on the bishop's voice as he read, district by district, the
names of the parishes and, after each, the name of the minister who was to serve it during the following year. Usually
my mother and sisters and brother did not know until we
reached home the next day whether we were to continue
living where we were for at least one more year or whether
we should be living perhaps two hundred miles away.

If a move was called for, it was necessary to act quickly.
As I recall, ten days were allowed for the transfer. This fast
change was possible at all only because the parsonages were
furnished (after a fashion!), and only our personal effects
needed to be transported. Even so, moving was no small job.
I have already mentioned several of the changes we were
called on to make. We lived in Listonburg, Pennsylvania,
Strasburg, Virginia, Frederick, Maryland, Pine Bluff, Arkansas, Stephens City, Virginia, Shepherdstown and Lewisburg,
West Virginia—all within fourteen or fifteen years. My father's last appointment was to a church in Baltimore, where
we were living when his death ended his career in what the
Methodists accurately call "the itinerancy."

It will be apparent from all this to what extent our life
was dominated by the institutional church—the presiding
elders and particularly the bishops. Except in one instance
perhaps, my father was never consulted about a prospective

change, and then, I think, he was simply informed in advance of it. But such was his attitude of loyalty toward "the conference" and "the bishop" that he never thought of raising a question as to either their rights or, except rarely, their wisdom. But his life, and therefore ours, so far as times and places of residence were concerned, were in their hands. "The conference" was our institutional environment—much more closely and significantly than was city, state, or nation.

But if we were thus almost physically *surrounded* by the church, it was also true that the church—this time, the local parish—was the *center* of our life, wherever we resided. My father, except for the care of his home, was almost fully preoccupied with its service, and the interests of his family as well were gathered around it. My younger brother has written a partly fictionalized book about our family in the early years, which he called *Sunday's Children*. It is a good title, but only if "Sunday" is understood as a symbol of the institutional church. We were the church's children, not alone on Sundays with its two or three services of worship to be attended, but on all the other days as well. This was true of us as a minister's family in a special sense and degree perhaps; but it was generally true of the inhabitants of the little towns in which we lived.

Sometimes Catholic Christians make a distinction between the inclusiveness of Catholicism, all of life falling within the horizons of the church, and what is regarded as the particularism and exclusivism of Protestantism. Such a distinction, if I am thinking of my boyhood and youth, seems irrelevant and untrue. No Roman Catholic town, say in France or Italy, could have been, even a century ago, so completely oriented to the church as regards its norms, its manners, and its habits of life, as were the villages and countrysides in which we lived. It mattered little whether the inhabitants were Lutherans, Episcopalians, Presbyterians, or Methodists, or indeed how they may have been divided denom-

inationally. Life within the town was life, if not within the
church, then under its shadow. There was still a Christendom, and our family knew itself as very much a part of it.

But far more important in our home than the church as
an institution was the personal piety in which we were
nurtured. Here, as will already have appeared, it was my
father who exerted the determining influence. My mother
was a Christian, as all her family had been and continued
to be, faithfully observing the forms of the church and doing
so with a genuine sense of their inner meaning. But it was in
my father's experience that this inner meaning was vividly
seen and deeply felt as the whole meaning of human life—
the source and ground of it, the reality and substance of it,
the purpose of it, the end and issue of it. His was the
creative spirit; or, better said, it was in him that the creative
Spirit made its presence indubitably known. His body was
frail and vulnerable. It is not surprising that when he was
scarcely fifty it succumbed to a ravishing disease. But his
faith was strong and invincible. It burned in him, a steady
glowing flame, a source of warmth and light to all about him
and especially to those who belonged most closely to him.
His piety was not blatant or obtrusive—there was nothing
of the fanatic or bigot about him—but it was there and,
like a living fire, it was irresistibly contagious. I have said
that no one who knew my father could fail to love him. It is
quite as true to say that no one who knew him could miss
the Spirit's presence. Perhaps these are not two statements,
but one.

Chapter 2

Life at School

FROM A VERY early age I had been committed in my own mind to entering the church's ministry. I do not recall ever considering any other occupation. I was perhaps twelve or thirteen years old when, in a clearly remembered pause or rest stop as my father and I were hoeing in our vegetable garden in Stephens City, I told him of my sense of vocation. This confession of my purpose came in answer to some question of his but was not the result of any urging, either then or earlier. As regards this "call," I have never wavered. I have always known, and know still, that God intended me to be a priest, although I should not always have used that term.

At the time of this conversation in the garden I was probably in my first or second year of high school. Stephens City had what was, I have every impression, an excellent elementary school but had no high school. The nearest such school was in Middletown, some five miles south on the famous Shenandoah Valley Pike, which ran immediately in front of our home. When I say "immediately," I mean precisely that. Only the brick sidewalk separated our front door and narrow porch from "the pike"—"famous" because it was reputed to be the longest stretch of paved road in the nation, extending from Winchester, seven or eight miles north of us, to Staunton, some eighty miles to the south, where "the valley" was thought of as ending.

As I recall, I had two years of schooling in Stephens City, taking the sixth and seventh grades there, and therefore it must have been only during the last year of the three we spent in Stephens City that I attended the Middletown high school. But I can hardly believe the period was so short as this, so vividly do I remember it and so important does it seem in my life. It was no small thing in those days to go five miles to school. School busing—or for that matter a bus—had not even been thought of. A friend in Stephens City of approximately my age began high school with me, and we usually made the trip there and back together on our bicycles. There was a period—my impression of how long is very vague—when my friend's father took us in his car, one of the two automobiles in the town. There were also days when, for whatever reasons, I was forced to walk to school. And at one time in the heart of winter when the snow was so deep on the pike that any but horseback travel was impossible, I recall riding to Middletown behind my father on our horse and his finding a home there where I might be a paying guest for the three weeks the emergency was to last. This experience was my first of being away from both my parents, and I remember with the poignancy of childhood impressions my feelings of its strangeness.

The Middletown school was, as I thought of it, an extraordinarily good one. As a matter of fact, I cannot even now conceive of a better. I remember especially the teachers of history, of English, and of Latin and mathematics, and I do not believe I have ever been more competently taught. Latin was, as one would expect, an entirely new subject to me, and I was fascinated by it.

At the end of the year my father was moved to Shepherdstown in West Virginia, some twenty miles or so north of Stephens City, still in the Valley of Virginia and not far from Harpers Ferry, where the Shenandoah pours into the Potomac. But the interruption in my schooling was not as hurtful as it might have been, for in Shepherdstown, too, I had excellent instruction at Shepherd College, a public preparatory and teacher training school located there. I remember with gratitude and affection my teachers in English and German and, again especially, my teacher in Latin.

Without completing my high school course, I qualified by examination for college entrance, and in the fall of 1916 J was admitted to Randolph-Macon College at Ashland in Virginia. My father accompanied me by train on my first trip there, and saw me enrolled and established in my room on the campus before going on himself to take care of some business or to make some visit in the neighborhood of Richmond, twenty miles to the south. I cannot describe how lonely his departure left me. I was fifteen and away from home in a strange place for what seemed an indefinite period. Moreover, hazing was the fashion of the time, and it was the major occupation of sophomores and many upper-classmen to make freshmen as miserable as possible, especially when they first arrived. I kept to my room as constantly as possible to avoid any unnecessary contact with my tormentors. After a few days of this I was almost unbearably homesick. One of the happiest and most vivid memories of my life is of hearing one afternoon a sound at the door of my retreat and of looking up to see my father entering. I had not expected him again and he had not expected to return. But some instinct had led him to know that I might need him. He spent only an hour or two with me and then resumed his journey. But that short interlude of love and home changed everything for me. My homesickness was gone, never to return, despite the troubles I continued to have.

My room was one of eight in an exactly square and absolutely plain two-story wooden building, referred to as a "cottage." A toilet serving the eight residents was attached outside at the rear. There were only four or five of these structures still standing from an older period, the majority of the students now being housed in two large brick "modern" dormitories. But a cottage room was less expensive and therefore for me a necessity. My furniture, according to invariable custom, was inherited or bought for a song from the preceding occupant. Along with a bed, a small clothes chest, a study table and chair, and a washstand, it included a small sheet-iron stove.

Running along back of the row of cottages was a long low building divided into sections to make a series of woodsheds, one for each room, and a first necessity for a new tenant was buying his wood for the winter, having it sawed to the proper length, and stowing it away in his shed. The big dormitories had central heating, but I soon discerned that this was a dubious advantage. The heat often failed when it was most needed. Many times during the long winters I was grateful for my ability to control the temperature of my room. No weather was too cold for my little stove. I would place a short log in it at night and close the draught. Waking early, as I always did with work to do (for I have never worked at night), long before the heat in the dormitories was turned on, I would spring from my bed, quickly close the window, open the draught of the stove and get back under the warm covers. In ten minutes the stove would be red-hot and my room comfortable.

I can hardly say that my college experience was a happy one. I have said that I qualified for admission at fifteen. This is true as regards academic requirements. But, in what are more important ways perhaps, I was not qualified at all. I was very much the introvert, very shy, poorly adjusted to the rough and tumble of college life even under the best circumstances. The obtrusive, aggressive attentions of many of my fellow students, not to speak of the brutal physical punishments and the even more brutal mental tortures, were to me peculiarly painful. As this fact about me became more and more apparent, the attentions and the efforts to subdue what was interpreted as my pride increased in constancy and intensity. This process went on throughout my freshman year, and my bad reputation continued to plague me in the following years. For a small part of this time I was to a degree supported and consoled by the presence at the college of three brothers from Winchester, Virginia, Wilmer, Paul and Amos Shryock, whose family belonged to one of the rural churches in my father's Stephens City parish and with whom I had already been somewhat acquainted. But though Amos was to become my oldest and closest friend, neither he nor his brothers could be of much help to me. Not till my senior year did I begin to feel some freedom.

I do not need to say that I was relatively uninvolved in the extracurricular life of the college. If I did not exclude myself, I was simply excluded. But in one rather important phase of this life I did take an active part. Students belonged almost automatically to one of the two literary societies, the Washington and the Franklin. The societies met every Saturday evening, and a brick building, as old as any of the college buildings, housed them on its first floor. They met on opposite sides of a corridor in large square carpeted rooms rather sumptuously furnished with desks resembling those of the members of Congress, the president's larger desk standing augustly on a raised dais. It was all very impressive! And it was taken with a seriousness, even by the less serious students, which in perspective seems amusing.

At each meeting of the society persons were appointed to present a "declamation," to deliver an "oration," and to take designated parts in a formal debate. A member critic, elected each year as one of the officers, commented on the several performances. I recall the complete and horrified silence which followed the one and only appearance of my friend, the irreverent and delightfully exuberant Amos Shryock. He had been appointed for the "declamation" and his response was the recitation of these lines:

> Thome folkth thay I lithp,
> But then I don't pertheive it;
> Now lithen while I call the cat,
> "Here, puthy, puthy, puthy":
> Now, thee, I don't lithp.

The critic was at a loss to express the society's sense of outrage. Amos was never again named on the program. But although I enjoyed his performance and admired his courage, I did not share his attitude. I had been active in similar societies at Shepherd College and found this feature of Randolph-Macon life very congenial and challenging.

It may be wondered how my college course was financed since it will have been made clear that my father could give me very little help. He surely did all he could and sent me something each month. My tuition costs were very low because Randolph-Macon, as a Methodist college, made a liberal allowance for sons of Methodist ministers in the Virginia and Baltimore Conferences, which gave it substantial support; and tuition costs in those days even at their highest were low indeed by today's standards. The conferences also made some provision for assisting needy candidates for the ministry, and I received each year a small but greatly appreciated grant, partly gift and partly loan. I managed also to make some money at odd jobs.

I have no records as to what a college year usually cost me, but my memory settles on $300. This figure seem. now incredibly small. I do not recall at all what my room rent

was, but I do remember that I paid $17.00 a month for my
three meals at an unusually good boarding house run by a
Miss Sledd, the sister of a professor at another institution
whom I was later to know well and to whom I am greatly
indebted. Even so, it is hard to see how, with travel and
various incidental expenses taken into account, I could have
lived on $300; and I may well be mistaken in that figure.

The First World War had begun in 1914, and midway of
my college career our own country became involved in it.
A Student Army Training Corps (SATC) unit had been
formed on our campus, and all of us were caught up into
the training program. We were given uniforms with a characteristic insignia; daily drills took place on our athletic
field; and there were other changes in our routine to remind
us that we were at war and that we students were very
much a part of it.

In the summer of 1918, an officers training program was
initiated at Plattsburg, New York, and designated students
from colleges over all the country, or at any rate the eastern
part of it, were invited to come there for an intensive three-
months course leading to a second lieutenant's commission.
I was one of a half-dozen Randolph-Macon students chosen
for this program. Having just finished my junior year, I was
on holiday at home in Lewisburg, West Virginia, where my
father had been recently moved from Shepherdstown. I recall
our excitement, and the consternation of my mother, when
the telegram arrived from Dr. Blackwell, the president of the
college, informing me of my appointment and instructing me
as to where to join the other members of our contingent for
the trip to Plattsburg. I felt I had no alternative to accepting
the appointment and my father reluctantly agreed with me.
My mother was strongly opposed but not ready absolutely

to forbid. At any rate I joined my associates, and two days later arrived, soiled and utterly exhausted from day-coach travel, at Plattsburg.

We were assigned beds in a large barracks, and the process of induction began. All went smoothly and well with me until I was asked my age. I told the examining officer that I was seventeen. He said, "Walk around the table, and I believe you will realize that you are eighteen." Of such an action I was absolutely incapable. I do not mean to be claiming any virtue; as a matter of fact, it may be argued that if I believed it was my duty to become a soldier, I was being only stubborn. But however my refusal be judged, it was not in my nature to sign my name to a statement I knew to be untrue. Several officers tried to persuade me; but though I wanted to see the matter in their way, I simply could not.

Finally I asked to be referred to the commandant (or whatever was his title). I told him that my age was seventeen and that I could not bring myself to say otherwise; but I asked whether there were not conditions under which a boy of seventeen might be admitted to the program. He was very kind, agreed (at least in words) that I ought not to consider lying about my age, but firmly informed me that I could not be accepted. I wired Dr. Blackwell and my family to this effect, and a few days later was at home again.

As it happened, the Armistice was signed in the November following, so that even if I had been admitted at Plattsburg, my period of service would have been brief indeed. As times have worked out in my life, this was my closest, indeed my only, approach to military service. Too young for World War I, when World War II came, I was too old and too much involved with family responsibilities to feel any strong obligation to enlist although I believed even more strongly than before in the justness of our country's cause.

✤

It is strange, even to me as I think of it, that I have written so much about my Randolph-Macon experience without yet mentioning what was my chief occupation there, attending and preparing for classes. The reason, I suppose, is that I have little strikingly memorable to say. I can speak only with admiration of my professors, especially of those in the classical languages, where my major lay. But in general I do not remember my college instructors nearly so vividly as I do my high school teachers, nor with the same gratitude and affection. In my experience it was in high school rather than in college that the more decisive steps in my educational development occurred. I had far indeed to go—and still have!—but the lines of development had been determined before I went to Ashland. No crucial events in my intellectual development occurred there.

In view of the fact, however, that I was to become eventually a professor of New Testament, I can hardly avoid referring more specifically to my experience in one of my courses—the course in the Bible required of all freshmen. It was taught by Dr. Frank Day, a wonderfully attractive man, although I think nobody would have regarded him as a particularly able teacher. He was in later years to become one of my best friends, and I dedicated one of my books to him. He had been introduced—I believe at Yale—to historical method in Bible study and sought to impart that method and its results to his students, as of course he should have done. But not only was I unready to accept the method and its presuppositions; I was absolutely unyielding in my opposition. A mark of my immaturity, the continuing boyishness of which I have spoken, was a stubbornness, not only in holding firmly to my own judgments of fact and value, but also in being unable to tolerate without protest what I conceived of as important error in others, especially if I was in the position of seeming by my silence to share in it.

I could give many instances from my earlier home and

school life of this unattractive, no doubt often quite obnox-
ious, trait. My teachers in the grades and high school soon
learned that if they made a mistake gross enough for me to
notice it, their attention would surely be called to it. Because
I had good teachers, this kind of thing happened rarely; otherwise, they could not have had the generally good opinion
of me, and I, the warm relations with them which, generally
speaking, prevailed. But there were the exceptional times. I
recall an incident at Shepherd College when I was perhaps
fourteen. Another student and I were to recite, or enact,
before a school-wide, or possibly a public audience, the quar-
rel scene between Brutus and Cassius from *Julius Caesar*
(Act 4, Scene 3). Readers may recall Brutus's lines:

> I did send to you
> For certain sums of gold, which you denied me:
>
> .   .   .   .
>
> . . . was that done like Cassius?
> Should I have answer'd Caius Cassius so?

Our coach, the speech or "elocution" instructor, wanted me
to emphasize the word "did" in the first line: "I *did* send. . . ."
I demurred, pointing out that there was nothing to indicate
that the matter was in question or dispute, referring also
to the metric, or rhythmic, requirements. She insisted; I
refused. Angered by my obstinacy and insubordination, she
sent me to the principal—the only time in my school experience when such a thing happened to me. He asked
me what the trouble was all about, and I stated my case.
I don't know whether I persuaded him or not, but I heard
no more about the affair, and certainly on the great night
declaimed, "I did *send* . . . ." This time I was right. But,
needless to say, it was not always so. I believe it could be
said that when inwardly convinced I was in the wrong, I
quickly acknowledged my mistake, always with great embar-

rassment. But my obstinacy, all through my boyhood, even about small, unimportant matters, must often have made me hard to live with.

When I objected as I did to Dr. Day's teaching, I was surely not in the right. Still, I was not able to see this for myself and was therefore unable to go along with his suggestions and conclusions. And because they seemed to me so important in their implications for Christian faith, I could not silently hear them. I restrained myself as much as possible, for I had learned something of tolerance since my high school days, but there were inevitably clashes of opinion between Dr. Day and me. He spoke to me ever so kindly, and so did Dr. Blackwell, the revered and beloved president of the college, to whom Dr. Day had apparently reported my obtuseness and recalcitrance. But their representations, reasonable as they were as far as they went, did not convince me. I could not but feel that the acceptance of their method, if it were allowed fully and logically to work itself out, would mean the collapse of the whole Christian position. They insisted that this was not true, and obviously they were right. But because (I believe it is fair to say) they themselves did not clearly see *why* they were right, I was not persuaded. The historical method of Bible study had to be put in a religious and theological context in which they were not able to put it before I should be able to accept it. I am not seeking to defend myself. I am not at all proud of my performance—quite the contrary! I might have listened quietly and kept my own counsel, and if I had been older and wiser I should have done so. But I was neither as old nor as wise as a college student ought to be, and I acted in my own characteristic way. The final consequence was an action by the faculty which, I am sure, had never been taken before, and perhaps has not been taken since: I was excused from the required Bible course!

In the final and overall reckoning, however, I did well

in my college studies and received my A.B. degree with honors in 1919. My father made his second trip to Ashland, now accompanied by my mother, to attend the graduation events. For all three of us it was a proud and happy time.

In those years in our area the Methodist Church did not require seminary training for its ministers, and I had no convictions as to its necessity (and in the absolute sense I still do not). After graduation from college I was at once "admitted on trial" by the conference and by June of 1919 I had been given my first appointment. I was sent to a circuit of six small rural churches, very much like my father's first parish—and in the same mountain range, only that mine was in eastern West Virginia and his in western Pennsylvania. But with the kind of terrain and the wonderful people who inhabited it I was quite familiar, and I felt at home in my new situation. My early experiences of accompanying my father on his travels among his churches and their members had prepared me for preaching, as well as for dealing pastorally with people, as no amount of mere schooling could have done. Sweet Springs, West Virginia, which during the previous century had been a popular summer resort with a large hotel (now abandoned and dilapidated), was the "center" of my circuit, and I secured room and board in the home of one of the villagers. But I spent very little time in Sweet Springs itself. I was free of all family responsibilities and slept at least half my nights in homes scattered over the two counties in which my six churches lay.

I had bought a horse and buggy and shall always remember even the details of my experience with them on my first Sunday's itinerary, with morning, afternoon, and evening engagements at far separated places. The distances were so great, the roads so rough, and the mountains between the churches so formidable (with little or no grading of the roads over them) that I was very late for every engagement and realized that a buggy was only an encumbrance. I sold it during the next week and afterward traveled only by horseback. I think often of the long, lonely rides through the silent uninhabited country. I think of them with pleasure, though at the time they must often have been arduous and uncomfortable, especially in winter, when snows could be very deep and temperatures were frequently far below zero. The time I spent on this "charge" was a happy and very rewarding period of my life, short as it was to be. Relations of great mutual affection were established with many people—some in each of the church neighborhoods—and I became virtually a member of not a few families.

I hated to leave the Sweet Springs area, but at the end of a single year I was moved to Sudbrook, a small church in Pikesville, a suburb of Baltimore, where, as I have said, my father and our family lived during the final years of his life. Here, too, I was very happy in my work and in my relations with my parishioners. With several families among them I am still in touch, as I am with one family from my earlier parish. I shudder now to think of how inadequate a boy of eighteen, nineteen or twenty years was for the pastoral, administrative, and preaching responsibilities I had in these two parishes. But at the time I carried them with no lack of confidence and, I believe it is only true to say, with some effectiveness and success. After one or two years at Sudbrook, however, I began to feel a very keen desire for further training, and in the fall of 1921 I entered upon my professional theological course in the divinity school of Emory University in Atlanta, Georgia.

My Emory life was much happier than my college ex-

perience had been. I was now more nearly at the proper age
for college or university experience, and my work in the
pastorate had made me more ready for normal social living
than I had been at Randolph-Macon. My closest friends and
associates at Emory, because they were nearer my own age,
were likely to be men in the college rather than the seminary—men like James Dombrowski, Foster Barnes, Ernest
("Pomp") Colwell, George Morgan, and Ebert Van Buren
(who later married my sister Virginia)—though I had many
friends in the divinity school, too. I was active in student
affairs, joined a fraternity, was a member of the glee club,
took part in several dramatic productions, and during one
of my years was the editor of the university yearbook.

I had in my divinity course at least three professors of
distinguished scholarship and competence, Professor Andrew
Sledd in New Testament, Professor Plato Durham in church
history, and Professor Warren A. Smart in biblical theology.
It is not surprising that after my college major in the classics,
I should find my interest centering in New Testament studies,
particularly since instruction in them was of so superior a
kind. Dr. Sledd was qualified, as my college teacher (for all
his excellence in many ways) had not been, to interpret
the historical method of Bible study in a way which enabled
me, not only to accept it, but also (as I should have had to
do if I was to accept it at all) fully to embrace it. He did not
accomplish this for me, as I see things now, by offering
an adequate rational theological substitute for the assurance
the acceptance of the Bible's verbal authority had given me—
this, or something like this, was to come later, and no doubt
I shall be speaking of it in this narrative. Rather, Dr. Sledd
himself manifestly had, in his own experience, so firm and so
vital an assurance of "things unseen," and this without any
such external authority as the Bible's mere words, that my
previous assumptions could not fail to be challenged. I was
forced to recognize that this same assurance on *our* part—my

father's, my own, and the community's in which I had been nourished—did not in fact rest on this support, despite all the strength of our conviction that it did. We had obviously been mistaken in our understanding of our own religious experience, and had identified as "fundamental" and essential in it an element—namely, the belief in the Bible's inerrancy —which was in fact, even for us, not only unnecessary, but really alien.

Needless to say, this conclusion was not reached without a great deal of inner struggle. And when it came, it was a by-product of an experience which, though precipitated by this struggle, had much wider and deeper implications. I was walking very late on a spring night along Briarcliff Road (and in those days it was in fact a road, not the street it has become), returning alone to Emory after a long conversation with a friend in the city about some of the problems of faith which were perplexing us both. The air was clear of mist or cloud. There was no moon, and the wide sky was brilliant with stars. Suddenly there broke in upon me with overwhelming power a realization of the awful beauty and the sheer immediacy of God. I felt at once an indescribable ecstasy and an almost incredible peace. The whole world became for a moment one vast delicious music. If I have ever had what could be called a single "conversion" experience, it was this. I could never again doubt God's reality or feel that it could be made subject to question by anything that could happen to me or others or by anything I might discover or find true.

The bearing of this experience upon the tension I had been suffering over the problem of the Bible's authority is too obvious to need remark. But only one who has had the kind of religious background I have described and who has been forced to face the terrible threat which biblical historical criticism seemed to pose to everything one held precious and inviolable, to everything which gave final meaning and purpose to human life—only such a person can realize the release and relief I knew. The door to a new freedom and a new peace had been opened—a peace between mind and spirit and a freedom to accept truth, whatever it might be, without fear. It was nothing less than "newness of life."

My senior year at Emory had only just begun when I was called home to Baltimore because of my father's final illness. It would be almost a full year before I should be able to return.

Chapter 3

Doubts and Searchings

MY FATHER'S DEATH occurred in January of 1924. At that time my sister Virginia was to finish her degree at Goucher College the following June, and Eva was to graduate from a normal, or teacher-training, institution also in Baltimore. I had come home to serve my father's parish as best I could during the last months of his illness. After his death the ecclesiastical authorities permitted me to continue in his place till my sisters should have completed their courses and could thus become self-supporting. Before the autumn they both found positions in the public schools of Winchester, Virginia, and my mother and my younger brother, now about fourteen years old, moved there with them. The home of my friend Amos Shryock and his wife Elizabeth was generously opened to them, and they occupied several rooms in their large old house as an improvised apartment. I returned to Atlanta to complete my own interrupted course and to hold concurrently a teaching position in the religion department of Emory College, which enabled me to support myself and to be of some help to the family.

Our separation, however, proved to be of short duration. After one year, my sisters secured teaching positions in Atlanta, and they and my mother and brother joined me there. I had then graduated from the seminary, but was to continue in my teaching work at Emory for another two years. The family proved to be more permanently located. Both of my sisters were destined to be married in Atlanta, and Virginia and her husband are still settled there. My mother made that city her home until her death, more than thirty years later.

For me, as will have appeared from what I have written about the relationship between my father and me, his death was a crushing, almost a devastating, event. And it will not be considered strange that a number of years were required for the recovery of the stability I had had before. Perhaps I never recovered just the same stability; and perhaps it is well that I did not. I was probably *too* dependent on my father—more dependent than he would have wanted me to be. His death forced on me a "release" which I did not want, for which I was not prepared, and which I would not be able fully to accept for some years. And yet I would not exchange that dependence—as it lives in my memory and as, in a sense, it continues—for any conceivable freedom from it. Such "freedom" would be separation from myself and therefore not my own freedom at all.

Dependence upon others does not need to be the merely limiting thing it is often thought to be. If it is true that belonging totally to God, if such a state could be attained by us self-centered men, would be "perfect freedom," it is also true that a certain kind and measure of belonging to others not only does not need to be incompatible with such freedom as it is possible for us to have but may be essential to it. For can one have freedom without loving? And can there be loving without some measure of dependence? But however that may be, the shock of my father's death was great indeed, and the adjustment to the fact of it was difficult. Some of what I had thought were the secure foundations of my life were severely shaken. I entered upon a period of uncertainty and vacillation which in retrospect seems far longer than the five years it actually lasted.

I have said that after my experience on Briarcliff Road I was never again to doubt God's reality. That is true; and this trust in God's being and presence was not assailed even in this time of testing, at any rate directly. The question, "Where is God?" did not trouble me. I knew he was *there,* as he had always been and would always be. But I could not put down the agonizing question, "Where is Father?"

I remember a brief conversation with my mother only a short time after his death in which she asked me that very question: "John, what do you believe has happened to your father?" And I remember the anguish I felt in being able to give her no other answer than, "Mother, I don't know." The anguish was there because I knew that her question went to the basic issue and that she understood my answer as doing the same. Neither of us was speculating on *where* or *how* he was, but was questioning whether he was at all. To me the hope of man's immortality had always been a corollary of trust in God's love. He who in love had created us— and created us with the capacity of receiving and in some measure returning his love—would not in the end destroy us or suffer us to be destroyed. So I had always felt and thought. I had witnessed death many, many times and had comforted, or tried to comfort, many bereaved persons with such words as these, and had done so with complete conviction. This fact made all the more shocking the discovery that when now for the first time *I* was the bereaved person, when death had taken from sight one with whose life *my own* was so closely intertwined, this deep conviction was shaken.

Perhaps this failure, or near-failure, of hope would have occurred in any case, but I cannot help thinking that its happening was made the more likely by the manner of my father's death. His death did not come to him suddenly, with his full personal powers intact, but by slow, quite imperceptible stages. From day to day, from week to week, we were watching the very process of his dying. The last month of his life was spent in a coma. It was always afterward a great consolation to us that not more than a few moments before the last of his faint breaths he miraculously awoke long enough to receive a kiss from each of us and with a look tell us good-bye as we stood weeping around his bed. But even so, can any hope of immortality be more strongly tested than under circumstances like these? The gradual attrition of our hopes and beliefs is more deadly than any sudden battering they may suffer. My hope was never completely lost and by the grace of God was fully revived. But not at once. It had gradually failed; only gradually did it return. And until it returned, I could not be secure. Faith in God, however strong and steady, could not be fully Christian, and to me at least fully satisfying, if hope was not equally steady and strong. St. Paul must have felt in this same way: hope belongs, with love and faith, to the essential reality of Christian existence—"these *three* abide."

I have said that for the greater part of the first three of these five somewhat troubled years I was teaching at Emory and living with my mother and sisters and brother. An episode during this period, which may appear to many trivial or absurd, was of the greatest importance both in my growth as a person and for the character of my later reflection as a theologian; and I cannot avoid recounting it.

Closely associated with me in my teaching was my dear friend, Ernest (or "Pomp") Colwell; in fact, he and I together constituted the Religion Department. We were much together and had frequent talks, not only in planning and carrying on our work, but also about more personal matters. In the course of several of these personal conversations we had expressed our common and growing dissatisfaction with ourselves as professing Christians. Our norm was the ethical ideas and example of Jesus. These we were engaged daily in studying and teaching, but we were now facing together how far we ourselves were from really accepting and following them. But why, we asked each other, should we not do so? We could not find any reasonable or satisfying answer to this question and decided that we would make a serious attempt at really being Christians.

I do not remember just how Pomp worked out in his mind what such an attempt would involve, if indeed I ever knew in detail. But there is no chance of my forgetting how the problem and answer shaped themselves in mine. What God required was that I give myself entirely to his service, which was the service of others; and this meant that those in greatest need had the first claim on me. But what was meant by "giving myself"? I reflected that I had twenty-four hours of time each day and a certain financial income each month. I was aware that important ethical questions could be raised as to the economic system through which my income reached me, and that I was obliged to do what I could to improve it. But there was an inevitable vagueness about this. More immediate, entirely definite, and quite inescapable was the fact that a certain amount of wealth reached my hands from my job and that after doing my part in providing for my mother's modest needs, I could wholly control the use I made of it, as I could also of my time. To devote myself to others, therefore, meant spending every moment and every dollar in conscious, deliberate service to others' needs. I decided to try to do so.

I was amazed to realize, once I had embarked on what amounted to a radically new way of life, how much of my time had formerly been spent carelessly, casually, thoughtlessly—not necessarily with selfish purpose, but rather with no conscious purpose at all. I had rested when I did not really need to rest; I had loafed or chatted with family and friends, or played cards, or read an entertaining book, or listened to music, or gone to a movie for no other reason than that I had nothing else to do. The same kind of thing, I realized, had been true of my way of spending my money. I had paid for useless amusements, for small luxuries, for unneeded items of food or drink—spending a relatively small, but significant, part of my small income thoughtlessly and carelessly, even if not consciously selfishly.

But, I argued with myself, although such thoughtless, "natural," use of time and money might under certain hypothetical circumstances be justified, could it be condoned at all in the world as it actually was—a world in which there was so much desperate human need? As I followed my new way, seeking to use all my time with deliberate helpful purpose, my experiences strongly confirmed the negative answer to this question which I had originally given on more theoretical grounds. Having to employ my time usefully, I sought out some of the more direly needy places. I discovered that so short a period as a half-hour, which I might have spent in idleness or in some trivial occupation, could mean the difference between life and death for some poor man in the charity ward of the city's public hospital who was literally dying because he could not pay for a necessary blood transfusion. Moreover, there were enough such poor men and women in the same need to use up every possible half-hour and every pint of blood any number of men such as I might have to bestow. I found a little girl living with her widowed mother in a shack in a cotton mill "village" in our city for whom a half-dollar of my money, which might have been spent for an idle hour or so in a movie house, or in treating a well-fed friend at a soda fountain, could mean a day's food which otherwise she would, literally, not have had. Furthermore, there were enough little girls and boys in similar poverty to exhaust the supply of unneeded, carelessly spent, pennies and dollars of thousands such as I.

All of this being true—and I knew it was—purposeless living seemed scarcely distinguishable from deliberately selfish living. And this could be said, not only of one's living in its general, overall character, but also of every small part of it. For every small part—every half-hour and every half-dollar—could mean a vital, crucial difference to some desperately needy human being, a human being not at all hard to find if one was seeking him. It was true, I recognized, that from the point of view of one reflecting on the massiveness of the total human tragedy, even in a limited area like Atlanta, what I was doing was very small indeed, scarcely worthy of note. But I daily discovered that from the point of view of some individual sufferer the value of the "cup of water" I could give was very great indeed—perhaps nothing less than life itself.

For several months I followed the way of life thus marked out. They were months of great spiritual joy to me. No longer was I merely talking about being a Christian. I was, I felt, being one. The truth that the truly and fully joyous life, the life of heaven, must be the entirely selfless life was borne in on me with irresistible force; and I was having at least a foretaste of that joy. My mother and sisters and my friends (I think especially of my dear friends the Stephens and the Davisons) were troubled about me, and I comforted and reassured them as best I could. I tried to explain the reasoning back of what seemed my strange conduct and of my apparent neglect of them and to communicate something of the heavenly satisfaction I was finding, at the same time wishing to share it with them. But no effort on their part to persuade me to abandon my way of life had the slightest chance of success. What I was doing seemed theoretically sound, and my actual experience was confirming its validity.

And yet eventually, needless to say, I did abandon it, as

Pomp did also. He would need to make his own confession; but as for myself, I abandoned it, not because I wanted to or decided to, but because I had to. I broke down under the pressure of it. I found out that the human frame, at any rate my own human frame, was not built to stand the strain of a total moral commitment. I do not mean that the commitment led me to neglect my physical health or to ignore or discount the body's needs. I had seen to it always that I had enough sleep and enough food of the proper sort. To stay well was an important part of my duty to others. My purpose required it. But there's the rub—"my purpose"! The "breakdown" was not a physical or nervous breakdown in any sense or degree, but simply a moral one. I could not stand the strain of so unremitting a moral demand, or, for that matter, so exalted a moral elation as I had been living with. I was forced to conclude that what I believed, with what seemed to me to be an irrefragable logic, I *ought* to do—this I *could* not do.

I am sure I do not need to speak at length of the disillusionment that ensued. The very certainty of my conviction and intensity of my commitment made it one of the most shocking experiences I have ever had. The ethic of Jesus was impracticable! What could I now trust? And how could I continue to teach, or preach, what I now had been compelled to acknowledge could not be practiced? Although the first acute effects of my failure passed in a few months, the question it left continued to be deeply disturbing. It was to be several years before I was able to find an answer to this problem which was in any degree satisfactory.

Another source of insecurity during this period was vocational indecision. It was not that I had any doubts about my calling as a minister; but I was increasingly perplexed as to whether my work was to be done in the parish or in the school. I was on the whole inclined to think that a teaching career was the more probable. If it was to be so, however, I knew I needed to be better prepared, and I began to think of further graduate study. But then came the question: In what field should the study be done? My academic experience thus far had prepared me best for work in New Testament, and my purely academic interest seemed to point in that same direction. But I also had an active concern about philosophical and theological issues; and often, as I reflected on the matter, these seemed more important than the problems of an ancient literature and history. And even further complicating the dilemma was the fact that the experiment in living which I have just now described had opened my eyes to pressing human needs and to social injustices for which, I was sure, the church had heavy responsibility. Should not my further studies, then, lie in the field of Christian social ethics?

A strong pressure in this last direction was provided by an experience I had in the summer of 1926. I had heard of a European travel-study seminar which Sherwood Eddy had been conducting during the summer months for many years. I decided early in 1926 that I should like to join it in the coming summer. I was by no means assured that I would be admitted, for Eddy insisted that only persons in position to make effective use of the experiences of the seminar in the influencing of public opinion and policy in this country should belong to it, and I knew that I had small claim to such a qualification. Still, I did apply and was accepted.

I discovered, when we gathered in New York before taking the *Berengaria* next day for England, that there were indeed many distinguished persons in the group, although there were enough people as obscure as myself (but none, I think, so young), to prevent my feeling uncomfortable or out of place. Among the more distinguished were several well-known ministers, such as Bromley Oxnam, the president of Du Pauw University and later to become a Methodist bishop; Ashby Jones, the eminent Baptist minister in Atlanta whose church I regularly attended but whom I had never seen before except from the pew; Mordecai Johnson, who was then the pastor of a church in Huntington, West Virginia, and was that very summer elected president of Howard University in Washington; and Justin Wroe Nixon of the Brick Presbyterian Church in Rochester. Kirby Page was also in the group, a long-time friend and associate of Mr. Eddy, and almost as active and prominent as Eddy himself, both as speaker and writer, in furthering the social gospel movement which Rauschenbusch had inaugurated and which was growing rapidly in strength and influence. There were others of the same order of distinction, two of whom I shall be mentioning soon in another connection. By the time we reached England, Mr. Eddy had asked me to be his roommate, and the consequent experience of intimacy with him meant, and still means, much to me.

We spent time in London, Berlin, Geneva (the League of Nations), Prague, Vienna and Paris. The programs Mr. Eddy had arranged in each of these cities were amazingly good, especially those in London, Berlin, Geneva, and Prague. We met leaders in political, economic, educational, and church affairs in every center. During our London stay of two weeks or so we were entertained by the prime minister, Stanley Baldwin, at 10 Downing Street, and by Lady Astor at her famous Cliveden estate, and had the opportunity of hearing them speak. We heard and discussed issues with such persons as Philip Kerr, who had been private secretary to Lloyd George and, as Marquess of Lothian, was later to be the British ambassador to the United States; Lord Thompson, a member of two Labor cabinets; Maude Royden and Studdert-Kennedy, influential churchmen; the scholarly political economist Harold Laski; and many, many others of similar note. Persons of corresponding stature addressed us and talked with us in the other cities. I recall especially Adolf Harnack and Paul Wolfson in Berlin and Manley Hudson and Salvador de Madariago in Geneva. The highlight of our Prague visit was a garden party arranged for us at the home of Thomas Masaryk, the beloved president of Czechoslovakia.

I do not need to say that this travel experience opened broad new vistas to my mind and greatly deepened the interest I had already begun to have in the issues of equality, justice and peace. Actually, it was this interest which led to the severance of my connection with the Emory University faculty. Although there had been objections from parents and alumni to my biblical views—and these no doubt contributed to forming the university's decision—it was a letter of mine to one of the local newspapers about the shamefully long hours and low wages in the cotton mills of the city and area which precipitated the action. Dr. Cox, the president of the university, called me to his office and, referring to the letter, informed me that I could expect no future employment there. In view of my growing concern about such matters, it is not strange that in this same period, early 1927, when I was contemplating graduate study, the field of social ethics should make a strong appeal.

I decided, however—and I believe correctly—that in the determining of where one will do intensive or advanced academic work, the most important consideration is, not what one rationally concludes is more important or most relevant, but rather what one finds most congenial to one's own mind. Therefore I finally decided on the New Testament, was fortunate enough to secure a fellowship, and entered the Divinity School of the University of Chicago in the summer of 1927 as a candidate for the Ph.D. degree in that field. But my start proved to be abortive. I was not yet sufficiently sure of my long-term professional goal to have a clear notion of what I was preparing for, and I left the university after two quarters of study.

Despite this abortiveness, however, the half-year in Chicago was not without great value. Besides the experience of being introduced to graduate study under very able teachers—study I was destined to resume and complete seven years later—there were important incidental and extracurricular benefits. On my European tour the preceding summer I had become particularly well acquainted with two of my fellow members of the Eddy Seminar. Dr. Charles Clayton Morrison was the editor of *The Christian Century* in Chicago. Emily Taft, besides being a most interesting and able person in her own right (she was the organizing secretary of the League of Women Voters in Illinois and was later to represent her state in the House of Representatives in Washington), had the distinction of being the daughter of Lorado Taft, the eminent sculptor. Because of the friendship between us—incalculably enriching to me for its own sake—I had had the privilege during the summer of meeting her father and of visiting under his guidance the art galleries of Paris and Florence. Both the Morrisons and the Tafts lived in the university neighborhood of South Chicago, and during my six-months stay I was a frequent guest at both homes.

I had many intimate and extended conversations with Dr. Morrison, who was one of the most brilliant men I have ever known and with whom I was to be more closely related some years later. Much of my leisure time I spent at Mr. Taft's large studio, a rambling building of many rooms just across the Midway from the university, where a number of young sculptors had, under his generous patronage and affectionate oversight, their own lodgings and workshops. Not only did I greatly reverence Mr. Taft and feel deeply grateful for his kindness to me, but I also found the companionship of the young artists most congenial and stimulating. I formed close friendships with several of them. Whatever appreciation of an informed kind I may have of the visual arts I owe to Mr. Taft, his daughter, and his pupils or protégé(e)s—and that is only a small part of my debt. These associations were a liberating and enlightening experience in many ways.

One other extramural experience, it occurs to me, deserves to be mentioned. Although it was a mere episode, it reveals at the very least something of my state of mind at the time. A few weeks after settling into my quiet and pleasant room at Goodspeed Hall on the university campus, I became quite uncomfortable in reflecting on how far removed I was from Chicago's poor and their needs. I visited Jane Addams, the wonderful woman who had founded and still directed Hull House on Chicago's west side, and tried to describe my feelings. I told her that I should have little time for service there but that I should like to rent a room at the House and thus be in some contact with its work and with the people it served. She generously acceded to my request, and I moved my trunk to Hull House. This happened in the hottest part of the Chicago summer; and my room on the second floor looked down on Halsted Street. I can recall nothing of my experience in it except the stench, the incessant noise, and the waves of heat pouring into my window, which in summer I had to keep open. If I had been actively engaged in the program at Hull House, I would have known compensations which, I hope, would have made these discomforts tolerable. As it was, I was quite unable to sleep, my work at school was suffering, and I had only the satisfaction of knowing that I was in some small measure sharing (though I could not feel helpfully or redemptively) in the bitter lot of Chicago's poor. After some weeks of this, I had to tell Miss Addams that I was simply not able to do what I had undertaken.

My failure was not unlike the failure I had realized after the more ambitious and thoroughgoing attempt at sacrificial living I had made a few months earlier in Atlanta. Indeed, my move to Hull House was really another and, as it proved, the final manifestation of the same mistaken conviction as lay back of the previous experiment—namely, that one can, by sheer force of will, live a redemptive life. The important phrase here is, of course, "by sheer force of will." George Eliot writes in *Adam Bede*, speaking of Dinah Morris's wonderfully healing help to a bereaved and very needy person: "From her girlhood upwards she had had experience among the sick and mourning, among minds hardened and shrivelled through poverty and ignorance, and had gained the subtlest perception of the mode in which they could best be touched and softened into willingness to receive words of consolation or warning. As Dinah expresses it, 'she was never left to herself, but it was always given her when to speak and when to keep silence.' " And then George Eliot adds, sharing more directly with us her own thoughts as she so often does: "And do we not all agree to call rapid thought and noble impulse by the name of inspiration? After our subtlest analysis of the mental process, we must still say, as Dinah did, that our highest thoughts and our best deeds are all given to us."

In other words, we act creatively, and therefore redemptively, only by grace. Any living, and life-giving, goodness we may have is not our achievement, or really our possession at all, but is God's gracious action in us. The discovery of this fact came to me only gradually and with any fullness or clarity only much later, but it had its ground and its dim beginnings in the failures of such attempts at deliberate goodness as I have described. My chapter in *The Christian Answer* (1945) and, more fully, my small book *The Ethic of Jesus in the Teaching of the Church* (1961) reflect these early experiences and their consequences. It was with good reason that I dedicated the latter book to Pomp Colwell, as "the long-time comrade in the search for answers to such questions as this book considers."

After leaving Chicago in December of 1927 and filling for a few months a temporarily vacant high school teaching position in Winchester, where I lived with Amos and Elizabeth as one of the family, I decided to return at least for a while to the pastorate. I accepted appointment as the minister of a small Methodist church in Bethesda, Maryland, a Washington suburb.

This pastorate in Bethesda, although it lasted only a year or perhaps eighteen months, marked a turning point in my life and presaged the end of the somewhat turbulent period which had begun with my father's death. The little church itself was a source of joy to me and I remember many of the people there with affection and gratitude. But what made the time most notable were two events, both in the spring of 1929—events not connected with Bethesda at all except in the sense that I happened to be there when they occurred. One of these was the offer, almost simultaneously, of two attractive jobs. The other was my engagement to Lois Bolles of Atlanta, to whom I was to be married a year later.

I had met Lois while I was for a few months the interim preacher at the First Christian Church in Atlanta during my student days. Soon after the beginning of my work there I had dropped in on a meeting of the Christian Endeavor, the church young people's society of those times, and had heard her speak. I was charmed by the beauty and vivacity of this slender blonde girl and deeply impressed by the character, the intelligence, and the humor revealed in her brief talk. Actually, I came as near to falling in love with her at first sight as, I imagine, is usually the case when that phrase is used. Afterward, I eagerly inquired who this girl was.

Lois was, I learned, the one daughter in a family of five long devoted to the parish—indeed, Mrs. Bolles's father had been its founder and first pastor. Lois was a student at Agnes Scott College in Decatur, a suburb of Atlanta. I made an early opportunity to meet her and a period of what should have been courtship began. We were both shy, but we made progress in knowing each other, and certainly my own admiration and affection for her were rapidly growing into a permanent romantic attachment. I suspected then, and later knew, that this was true for her, too. But all of this was near the beginning of the period of instability and turbulency I have described. Our intimacy was interrupted. Then came my European trip and later my Chicago stay.

But now at Bethesda I was finding myself again and in doing so was finding her. I realized that I had been in love with her, was in love with her now, and that, more than anything else, I wanted her to be my wife. By this time she had graduated from Agnes Scott and had also finished a post-graduate course in library science. She was one of the librarians at Emory University and was to become the head librarian at Agnes Scott the next year. I knew of her plan to attend a conference of librarians in Washington in the spring of 1929, and I resolved to take advantage of that occasion to make my avowal and proposal. I did so and she accepted me. Her stay in Washington was to last another few days, but I fear the librarians' conference saw little more of her!

As for the two job offers, the other notable event I mentioned as occurring during my Bethesda period, I was invited to become chaplain at Antioch College in Ohio, and a similar invitation came from Fisk University in Nashville, Tennessee. Both invitations were of a kind to interest me very much. In either institution I should have the opportunity of doing the work of a minister, to which I knew myself called, and at the same time of having a part in the work of higher education. I visited both institutions, being most cordially received by Dr. Arthur Morgan, the president at Antioch, and by Dr. Thomas Elsa Jones of Fisk. After these visits, there was no doubt in my mind as to where I wanted to go. At Fisk, in addition to the combined roles I have spoken of, I would have the inestimable privilege of exercising them in one of the very few interracial communities then existing in the South. Perhaps there I might escape the inner tension I had come acutely to feel as a member of a virtually white society. Perhaps there, not by overt or even conscious effort (such efforts had led to failure and disillusionment), much less by talking about race or "the race problem," but just by being myself and doing my work as I would be doing it wherever I might be, I might contribute, however slightly, to the better understanding between black and white and to the juster, more humane order which eventually must come.

I recognized, however, that accepting this Fisk University position would involve, on Lois's part as well as on my own, a sharing, as far as a white couple could, in the segregation of the Negro people and in the deprivation to which the Negro was subject. Worse than nothing, as I saw and felt it, would have been working on one side of town and living on the other. Such an arrangement did not even enter my mind as a possibility. Moreover, I knew that this sharing could not be genuine or creative unless both of us felt it as a privilege, and not in any degree whatever as a necessity or obligation. All of this being true, I knew I could not accept the position at Fisk without discussing the whole matter with Lois. I was soon assured that she felt as I did, and it was agreed that I should go to Fisk in the autumn of 1929 and that she would join me there as my wife a year later.

Chapter 4

At Fisk University

My term as chaplain at Fisk University is a minute episode in its history and is now forgotten by all but a very few. But its importance for me, then and now, cannot be exaggerated. I should be quite unable to describe my feelings of adventurous hope in going there, the joyous excitement and the deep satisfaction I knew in being there, and the wounding, never to be fully healed, which I suffered in departing. My total time at Fisk was only seven years, Lois being with me in six of them. But no period of my life, except my earliest youth, can compare with these Fisk University years in its critical meaning and effect—so fully was I committed to being there, so much of what I most deeply believed was involved in my being able to stay there, and so disturbing, therefore, so threatening to some of my dearest values, was the discovery that I could not. But what I mean in all of this cannot be quickly told. I must begin at the beginning, and that beginning for me lies in being the child of southern white parents, and of just such parents as mine were.

My father and mother had both belonged to families of what would be called in cultural (not in economic) terms the upper middle class. I am tempted to describe their attitude toward Negroes as the generally characteristic attitude of that class in the South of seventy-five years ago. But I am not enough of a historian to be sure such a description would be true or indeed to know whether any attitude could be called "generally characteristic" of any class. I do have some impression of the attitude of my parents and their families and of the other white people whom I most respected and by whom I was most influenced. How widely their views and ways were shared by others I shall not try to say. But I believe they were shared by many.

To describe this attitude or state of mind, however, is no easy task, and I shall make no attempt at any systematic analysis. Indeed, I am inclined to think one would need to be oneself a fairly intelligent southern white American man or woman, gently reared a generation or more ago, to know its true inwardness, and even such a person would no doubt take exception to my own, or any other contemporary, analysis or description of it. All such persons, however, would agree that it is quite false to judge, as many do, that this attitude was simply one of hostility and contempt. I do not recall a single expression of such an attitude in our home, and I am sure there could never have been one. The notion that the Negro was not a full human being, a child of God as every man is, could never have been so much as suggested among us. The idea that he was entitled to the same political and economic rights as other Americans would never have been questioned. There were warm, and I believe mutual, relations from time to time between us and at least a few Negroes. I can remember the cordial relations my father had with Negro ministers in some of the Virginia towns we lived in, recalling particularly the courtesy with which he greeted them. And again there was every indication that these relations were, certainly in some important ways, fully mutual.

At the same time, however, a "social distance" separating us and indeed all white people from Negroes was taken for granted. The reason the instances of my father's respectful and gracious receiving of the calls of the Negro ministers stands out in my memory is the rarity, and therefore to me as a child, the strangeness of these visits. I can remember talking with my father about this separation and his effort to justify it. He said that it was in the interest of both the black man and the white that they should follow separate ways and maintain their separate social communities. I recall feeling at the time that, while he had no doubt of the necessity of this separation, he felt some conflict between his acceptance of it and his Christian views, and that he was not altogether happy with the justification he offered. Why should the Negro minister, whom he called "brother" and whom he warmly received in the "parlor," not be welcomed also to the dining room? But questioning in any serious and sustained way the social order in which he had been reared and which he had always accepted without thought as being the order of nature was hardly to be expected. In the limited circle of his life the problem was not insistent enough to demand solution or even to require much attention. Still, I knew he was uneasy about how as a Christian he ought to act in his personal relations with his Negro brethren.

Many years later, long after his death, this early impression was confirmed through a conversation with my mother. I have referred to the occasional times early in my childhood when we had servants. We children did not then notice the fact that they were always white women. But later, long accustomed to Negro servants among our white neighbors, I asked my mother why it had not been so with us. She answered that "Mr. Knox" always insisted that our servants should be white because he was uncertain as to just how Negroes should be treated and therefore would have felt ill at ease in their constant presence. Having the impression I already had of my father's unsettled mind on this matter, I understood what she said to mean that he would have *wanted* to treat the Negro servants (as any servants) as "social equals," but that he felt so much under the command of the prevalent ethos in racial relations that he would have found intolerable difficulty in doing so. And, it is important to add, the crux of this difficulty would have been, not facing embarrassing social consequences, but being involved in an inner conflict which he was not prepared to resolve.

Whatever qualms in this regard my father may have felt, however, I must confess to having been quite free of such misgivings during my childhood and youth. I took the segregation system as a matter of course, with little thought either for the system or for those who suffered under it, in those times so patiently and quietly—*too* patiently and quietly! This was true of me during my school and college days. I cannot recall any discussion of "the race problem" or of the ethical issues in the current state of Negro-white relations, or indeed any signs of awareness among my fellow students and my teachers that an ethical issue was involved at all. I have every reason for thinking they were as insensitive as I. Indeed, has not the white South's great and tragic failure in this regard always consisted chiefly, not in intentional cruelty among the larger number of white Southerners, but rather in blindness to the gross inhumanity and the grossly dehumanizing effects of the segregation system, the immeasurable human costs of it, costs so great in suffering that, once they were seen, no rationalization of the system could ever have appeared anything but the specious thing it is? To put the case in this way is not, needless to say, to exonerate or condone. The "blindness" has always been half-conscious and half-willful, and therefore to a large degree a shameful and cruel neglect. Moreover, it has been this half-deliberate "blindness," this "shutting of the eyes," on the part of the more decent which has given encouragement, and in the end immunity, to the brutal and sadistic with their deadly cowing threats and their shameless acts of violent hatred.

As to just when I first became aware of the awful crime of the white man against the Negro and of my own sinful participation in it I am not at all clear. The realization came gradually and, I believe, had its beginnings during my first year at Emory. Among my teachers there, Dr. Smart was keenly aware of the grim realities and greatly concerned to confront his students with them. Dr. Plato Durham also was sensitive in this respect and was known to be active, along with Dr. Ashby Jones of the Ponce de Leon Avenue Baptist Church, and Dr. C. P. Wilmer of St. Luke's Episcopal Church, in the work of the Commission on Interracial Cooperation, which had been organized in the South only a few years earlier under the vigorous leadership of a white civil rights protagonist of those times, W. W. Alexander. In touch with these men as I was, I could not be long in realizing something of the gross injustice and inhumanity of the segregation system and in recognizing that something needed to be done for the breaking of its hold on black and white alike. For I could see that though it bore more overtly and more heavily upon the Negro, the white man just as surely was being crippled by it, and that this was not less surely true of him because he was so completely unconscious of what he was doing to himself in doing what he did to his brother.

As for definite action in this area, however, I do not remember any up to the time of the experiment in living on which Pomp Colwell and I embarked—or, in any special way, even then. It is true that some of the people at Grady Hospital to whom I gave blood were Negroes, but this only happened to be true. I recall, too, visiting from door to door among the poorer Negro families, but here again my interest was almost entirely in their poverty and only incidentally in their race. I can say, however, that by this time I was, so far as one can know such things about oneself, altogether free from my inherited prejudices and ready, even eager, to escape from their limiting effects.

My earliest opportunity of this kind came when in 1926 or 1927 I heard of an effort being made by a few students in the colleges of Atlanta, black and white (for in those days there were no mixed student bodies in the South), to organize an interracial group for discussion and better mutual acquaintanceship. I jumped at this opportunity and became an active member of the group. We met only at one or another of the Negro colleges—Morehouse College, Spelman College, or Atlanta University—for none of the white colleges, such as Emory, Georgia Tech, or Agnes Scott, was ready to permit meetings of this kind. These gatherings, leading directly and immediately to friendships with such Negroes as B. R. Brazeal, Herbert King, and Grace Towns, and through them, soon and later, to many others across racial lines, were incalculably significant to me. I realized that till then I had been living in only half a world, if indeed in even so much of it as that. A whole new dimension in being a person was revealed, and I found great freedom and joy in this larger personhood. I was inexpressibly grateful to these new friends who so patiently initiated me into this warming and liberating experience and opened themselves so generously to me. Not long afterward I had the chance to tell Mr. Alexander of my desire to live and work as a minister in an interracial community. And it was as a result of his initiative that, in the spring of 1929, the opportunity at Fisk University was offered me.

I was twenty-eight when in the fall of that same year I entered upon my work at Fisk. I arrived in Nashville a few days before the college session was to begin and settled into my quarters—a room in Bennett Hall, one of the old buildings on the campus, belonging perhaps to the era of the college's founding not long after the Civil War. It was then being used as a dormitory for freshmen men, and I tried to get acquainted with my fellow residents as they arrived. It was as well perhaps that these first acquaintances were newcomers like myself. We were strangers together, a fact which, I at least felt, made something of a bond among us.

I have spoken of the Fisk University constituency as an "interracial community"; and that in principle was true. Indeed, I am not sure that in the South of that period, outside a number of such scattered private colleges, there were any institutions at all of any kind in which blacks and whites were permitted to work together as equals. It must be said, however, that the interracial character of these colleges was at best of the kind now called "token"; and they were ordinarily called "Negro colleges." At Fisk all of the students— as I recall, about three hundred fifty—were Negroes; state laws forbade any white enrollment. The faculty, in the beginning made up entirely, or almost entirely, of white men and women from the North, had over the years become increasingly Negro, and in the period of my residence at Fisk was, as I recall, about equally divided between the two racial groups. But even so, given the number of black students and also the fact that the institution was located in an area of Nashville where only Negroes lived, the white contingent was a very tiny minority in the total community.

In retrospect I can only marvel at the confidence with which I entered upon my life and work. As I look back, I can see the difficulty—one might almost say, the enormity—of what I had undertaken. Here was I, a white man of less than thirty years, sharing in the guilt of generations of his ancestors, expecting to be welcomed into a community of Negroes and even presuming to accept a position of spiritual leadership in that community—a position offered, not by the community itself, but by the administrative powers of the university, most of whom happened to be white men like myself! How bold, how rash, could one be! If I had thought such thoughts as these or seen the matter in such terms, would I have been able to accept the position which had been offered me? But fortunately, for me at least, I did not look at it in just that way.

Not that I was thoughtless about the guilt. There was not a day of my seven years at Fisk in which I did not think of it, and it was the recognition of it and the desire to do something about it which had led to my seeking the privilege of membership in such a community as this. But my faith in human brotherhood, not simply as an ideal, but as a fact about man, and the actual experiences I had had of warm, respectful, and fully mutual relations across the racial line did not allow of doubt that, so great was the grace of God as it worked in men's hearts, I might be forgiven and accepted. My first Sunday at Fisk, one would surely suppose, must have been for me a tremendous crisis—facing this large congregation of black men and women who must certainly be alertly critical of this youthful white upstart. But so innocent was I of any such thoughts that I do not have any memories at all of that first day. By that time I had forgotten my color or my congregation's, and my experience of their kindness gave me confidence, not so much in myself as in the possibility of a life fully shared between us.

Each successive day increased that confidence. Gradually I became acquainted with the students, visiting the men in their rooms or inviting them to mine, and meeting all the students, men and women, more casually after church, at various social affairs, in the dining hall, in the corridors, or on the streets of the campus. It was not long before I was calling some of them by their first names. I recall that an older Negro with some official duties on the campus for a few weeks near the middle of that first year, hearing me address several of the girls by their first names, made some complaint about it. I learned of this only through one of the students who expressed her resentment at this interposition and assured me that she and the other students, men and women, whom I had begun to address so familiarly, fully understood my attitude toward them and were glad for it. This girl will never know—though I tried to tell her—how grateful I was for the reassurance she gave me.

Some of the students of that first year—and this would be true of all the later years as well—became my warm friends. With some of these this friendship has been constantly maintained or frequently renewed; others I have never seen or heard from since my Fisk days. I shall not attempt a list; it would be much too long. But I consider every person whose name is, or might be, on it as one of my most important teachers and benefactors and the friendship as one of my dearest treasures. It goes without saying that I had similarly warm relations with many members of the staff and faculty and the same grounds for gratitude.

My social life (and to anticipate a little, Lois's also) was virtually limited to the campus and to the relatively few Negro families nearby who attended the chapel or with whom, in some other way, we became acquainted. This was true, partly because the white community saw to it that it should be so, but also because we could not have felt comfortable in social relationships to which our friends were not also admissible. The same considerations prevented any use on our part of Nashville's public entertainment opportunities. We refused to be a willing part of any segregated white group. We could have climbed to the balconies of the local motion picture houses, but if we had done so, we should have found few if any of our friends, for most of the Negroes we knew preferred doing without movies to seeing them under such degrading conditions. The consequence was that social life on the campus was far more than ordinarily self-contained. We lived much to ourselves, having our work, our worship and our play largely together.

I was expected to do a little teaching, as professor of religion, but my chief work was that of chaplain, and my life had its center in the chapel. Each of my weeks reached its goal or culmination in the service there at eleven o'clock on Sunday. The chapel building was a somewhat rounded structure with a short steeple and contained little more than a single large room. Pews were arranged in a semicircle. Beyond them to the front was a raised platform on which the pulpit stood and, just beyond it, several of the big black pulpit chairs one used to see. And still farther, filling the entire front quarter of the room was the choir space—tiers of seats stretching the full width of the room and gradually rising almost half-way to the ceiling, each long row higher than the one in front of it. One of the most glorious things about Fisk was its tradition of music, and I feel sure this must still be true. There was an excellent school of music. Paul Cravath, member and sometime chairman of the board of the Metropolitan Opera Company, whose father had been the first president of Fisk, and David Mannes, founder of the Mannes School of Music, were only two of a number of Easterners who came regularly to attend the annual Music Festival. Roland Hayes, an alumnus, often visited us. In earlier years the university had been chiefly known through the Fisk Jubilee Singers, whose fame had been worldwide and who were still an active singing group. Only very occasionally did we hear them in the chapel; they were chiefly a touring ensemble. A very large portrait of the original Singers was hung above the choir on the wall facing the congregation.

No one would have argued with the statement that there was no finer vocal musical organization in Nashville, or probably in Tennessee, than our choir of perhaps a hundred

voices—indeed, none in the same class of excellence with it.
Its director was Ray Brown, the head of the music school,
who was later to be the much beloved teacher and conductor
of music at the General Theological Seminary in New York.
John Work, the well-known composer, was associated with
him. The service on Sunday was the familiar simple one of
the Congregationalists (under whose auspices Fisk was established), but the organist, Miss Glass, and the choir with
their sensitive and all but flawless renderings of Bach, Pales-
trina, and other classical church music composers gave it a
quite extraordinary character. The preacher was under a
severe challenge indeed if he hoped to speak words appropriate to, or even halfway worthy of, the exalted mood to
which the music brought us. Before the sermon the music was
invariably from the traditional or classical sacred music rep-
ertoire. But immediately after the sermon, some member of
the choir (usually John Work) without any announcement
sang the first words of a spiritual which at the moment
seemed to him appropriate. The always lovely melody was at
once taken up by the whole choir, and seconds later the entire congregation was singing it. And so the hour's experience
ended.

It was an awesome privilege to be the preacher in such a
service, and I gave a great part of my time to preparing my
short sermons. I wrote them all out with great care and in the
process virtually memorized them. In 1932 a number of them
were assembled and published as a small book, "He Whom a
Dream Hath Possessed." This was done on the urging of the
president and some other members of the congregation, and
whatever distribution the book had was largely owing to
their interest and efforts on its behalf. I knew then, and I
know even better now, that my sermons were not worthy of
the opportunity I had, or comparable in beauty and value
with what others were offering in the service; but I can truly

say that they were the very best offering my heart and mind could have made.

In June of 1930 Lois and I were married and after a summer in Europe (a group of students who lived in New York came to the ship to see us off), we began our housekeeping in a small two-story cottage which the university had built for us as one of several homes for new faculty members. There had never been any doubt between Lois and me that we wanted children, and (to anticipate a little) our lovely Jack joined us there in early 1932—the most joyous moment in our Fisk period. One of the other new houses, all of them nearby, was for Elmer Imes, the professor of physics, our dearest friend among my colleagues. Into another new house James Weldon Johnson and his wife Grace, who were also to become warm friends, came to live. But again I must restrain the impulse to name members of our small friendly community. I should not know where to stop!

It was, I confess, with just a little trepidation that I carried Lois across the threshold of our new home and thus across the threshold of a new world, newer than she (or any white person, certainly any southern white person) could have realized in advance. I had enough confidence in her and in that world to trust the outcome. And yet I could not feel absolutely secure. I myself had moved only gradually over a number of years—intellectually, morally and emotionally— toward an interracial life. I had had the experience of knowing and loving, on equal and mutual terms, more than a few Negroes. But she was leaving very suddenly and abruptly the white South in which she had always lived, and entering the black South—and the two Souths, despite their physical nearness to each other, were still two worlds, separated from each other by a gulf strangely wide and deep. No one, white or black, who knows the South of forty years ago—and the South of today is beginning to be significantly different— and who has any imagination at all can fail to realize the radical meaning of the step Lois was taking and the strength of the demands it made upon her own integrity, capacity for adventure and change, openness to truth, ability to understand others, good will, and tact.

I speak of all this, not to point to the "hardness" of the task she was undertaking. She was no more conscious of undertaking a "hard task" than I had been. We were both accepting a rich opportunity which, at that time at least, only a very few white persons enjoyed. My intention is rather, to pay tribute to the beautiful, wholehearted, and completely natural way in which she became a part of our community. She won her own distinctive place there and in the hearts of many of its members. When after six years we were forced to say good-bye to our home and work in Nashville, and to leave for a northern city, she wrote the following lines, which reveal, far better than I could say it, what our experience at Fisk had meant, and would always mean, to her:

To the South of My Birth
on Going Away

Let me not with easy tears take leave
Nor feign a sudden parting: six years ago
I fled in mind your septic pride of race,
Found strange, sweet refuge here within your borders.
Around my house your lavish gardens spread;
Aloft the mocking bird pours out his song;
But foreign is this place as lands abroad
To your provincial spirit. Here live a grace
And courtesy more true than once adorned
Your yet beloved prime. . . . Forgive your child,
No more in arrogance would I turn from you

Than with tears. Have I not heard those deep
But ever stronger stirrings of new life
Which yet may come to birth? And if they fail—
What other hopes may lie with them still-born!
Who dares to cast a stone these bitter days?

I find a note in James Weldon Johnson's hand on the manuscript of this poem: "This is very, very good and ought to be
published."

I have emphasized the positive elements in our relations
with other members of the university community—their gracious hospitality, their friendliness, their cooperativeness,
the warmth of many friendships. And in doing so I am indi-
cating truly the general or predominant character of our
experience. But what I have said must not be taken as meaning that there were no painful moments or occasions of
tension. Actually, there were not a few of them. If our years
at Fisk were extraordinarily happy years, they were also at
times, perhaps by the same token, extraordinarily painful,
too. A white person could not "identify," or want and try to
"identify," with the Negro in America a generation ago (and
probably still) and not know pain. And though most of that
pain would lie in his sharing (to the small extent a white
person can) in the Negro's peculiar griefs, he would have
peculiar occasions for grief of his own. Sometimes these
might arise from real failures on his part in understanding
and tact, for the white person who wished to be a part of a
Negro community walked, at any rate then, a very thin line.
All the good will in the world would not assure that he
would succeed. And yet one sure way *not* to succeed would
have been by careful watching and studied effort. Only the
most transparent sincerity combined with a most delicate

sensitivity to an extraordinarily complex human condition and state of mind could succeed in preventing a false step, and few if any white men could be so fortunate as never to make one.

But not all of the white man's difficulties in such a situation need to be ascribed to his own obtuseness or error, not to say prejudice. Negroes may have their own prejudices and their own failures in understanding. Given the long bitter history of the Negro people in America and the bitterness of much of their daily experience, it is natural that they should be, generally speaking, habitually critical and suspicious of white men, and it is almost inevitable that some should be intransigently hostile and cynical. The white man who aspires to equality with a black man carries a heavy burden of proof. How could it be otherwise?

I have spoken of the time during my first year when my practice of calling certain students, whom I had come to know well, by their first names aroused suspicion in certain quarters. I recall, to cite a trivial but illustrative incident, the pain I felt when early in that same first year I was told that some were saying that I had prolonged the period of prayer in the preceding Sunday's service in order to abridge the time the visiting preacher, my friend Howard Thurman, would have for his sermon—Howard being, needless to say, a Negro. I am not sure that the prayer was longer than usual; but should I have been so sensitive to others' sensitivities as to forestall such a criticism by making it unusually short?

Another incident very early in that same first year comes to mind in this connection. A white man whose name was much in the news as a poet and a speaker on literary subjects had come to Nashville to fill several engagements at other colleges in the city. One of my closer friends, a rather mature graduate student in sociology, in whom I had complete confidence (and still have; he is now a professor of sociology in a well-known college), came to me with the suggestion that I find out whether the poet could not include us in his schedule by speaking at one of the weekday assemblies, for which I had responsibility as well as for the Sunday service. I accepted the suggestion, called the man at his hotel, and arranged for his address. When the occasion came, his very first words revealed that, however knowledgeable he might be about literary subjects, he lacked even elementary intelligence and sensitivity in the field of human relations and was quite incapable of speaking inoffensively to such an audience as we were. I say the first words disclosed this, and I cannot remember a more uncomfortable time than the mercifully brief period which followed. It was uncomfortable for everyone, but it was especially uncomfortable—or, rather, uncomfortable in a special way—for me. In this case, I knew I had been at fault: I should have informed myself specifically on the man's experience in relationship with Negroes and with his attitudes in that area, rather than assuming, as I did, that a generally intelligent man would be intelligent there also.

I was never to make the same mistake again. But at the time I had to bear, at any rate for a while, the suspicion of some that I had invited the visitor because I was sympathetic with his views and shared his attitudes. Needless to say, it was because I was a white man that this interpretation could be put upon the incident. If I had been a Negro, no such thought would have occurred to anyone. My friend the sociology student felt as much regret and shame as I, but as a Negro he was, of course, not open to the same suspicion.

I shall recount one more incident of this same kind, much more painful to me because it involved Lois, and almost at the moment of her arrival. Fisk University had an excellent library, but at that time only one professionally trained worker in it, the librarian himself. Besides directing the library, he was scheduled to teach several courses in library science for students interested in the possibility of later taking graduate work in that field and eventually becoming librarians. Just before the beginning of the year when Lois was to join me, while she and I were in Atlanta, she received a letter from the university informing her that the librarian had been granted a leave of absence for the year, that arrangements had been made for assistants to carry on the work of the library during his absence, but that the intended provision for the library science courses had for some reason failed. It being known that Lois had had the professional librarian's training and also several years experience as a librarian, she was urgently requested to assist in the emergency and to teach the courses. She was exhausted and indeed not well after our long wedding trip and the exertions which had preceded it and was strongly disposed to decline this invitation. Not realizing how very tired she was and not knowing yet how very delicate her health was, and was always to be, I rather urged her to accept it, thinking that the work would help initiate her into the life of the community. She finally answered the letter with an agreement to do so.

When it became known that she was to teach the courses, a Negro member of the faculty, without our knowing it, saw in the arrangement an instance of discrimination against a Negro woman, an assistant on the library staff. Neither Lois nor I will ever forget a meeting held soon after we arrived and before the semester's work had begun. It was a meeting, as we recall, of the faculty at which new members of the teaching staff were to be introduced. Among them Lois was presented and officially welcomed. She remembers the very sentence in which she expressed her thanks and the joy she felt in being there.

But this happiness was due for a sudden and rude shock, from which it took her some time to recover. For the professor to whom I have referred took this occasion to denounce her temporary appointment in the boldest possible terms—indeed, in what must be regarded as intentionally wounding terms. Those who know her will not need to be told how deeply hurt she was by this brutal attack. The professor was unable, or unwilling, to see that competence to serve efficiently as an assistant to the librarian by no means qualified one to teach library science. He did not believe, or at any rate was unwilling to acknowledge that he believed, the official statement that the alternative to Lois's teaching the courses would have been simply the canceling of them. The discussion, increasingly acrimonious on his side, continued for some time. I do not recall that anyone except him and the president took part in it, but later there were many expressions of sympathy and encouragement for Lois, and after renewed hesitation she fulfilled the assignment she had accepted. I do not know whether the professor was ever persuaded that she did not seek the post, or if not, that it had been offered her for any other reason than that she was a white person. Certainly, although our relations with him continued to be not unfriendly, he never made any explanation or apology. But surely if there was ever a case of an unjust suspicion of another simply on the grounds of a racial difference, this was such a case.

All of these incidents occurred in my first year or at the very beginning of my second (Lois's first). I believe it is true to say that the harsher judgments were never the judgments of more than a few and also that as time passed such suspicions of us became even less frequent and less likely. But except within the growing circle of close friends, we could not help feeling the weight of what I have referred to as the "burden of proof." And this burden was not less heavy because we could understand only too well the good reasons why it was imposed.

In view of all the impediments to understanding and the

difficulties in mutual adjustment which might reasonably be expected, someone may ask how I could have justified my being at Fisk at all. Why should I have wanted to be there and on what grounds could I have thought it right and good that we be there? I suspect the professor to whom I was just now referring would have denied, not only the value, but also the propriety, of a white man's presence in such a community. And he would have been able to argue plausibly for his position. This issue will come in for some longer discussion a little later. But at the moment I shall say only that one's position on it will in no small part depend on whether one believes that there can be "liberty" and "equality" without "fraternity," as well as on whether one finds value in fraternity simply as such.

On the latter point I could have no doubt. My life could be only as deep and broad as the fraternity in which I participated. There was, I could not but feel, intrinsic and ultimate worth in the experience of human mutuality. I recall the shock I felt when not long after my coming to Nashville, I spoke to a white minister there about the tragedy of the separation between the white and black populations of that city and he asked, quite seriously and earnestly, "Why should it be considered a tragedy?" He might have agreed on the desirability and rightness of liberty and equality for the Negro, as for the white; but why fraternity between them? I wonder whether the protesting professor whom I have mentioned might not have asked the same question. Neither, it may be presumed, could see how much poorer he himself was because of the strictures society imposed upon his brotherly sharing.

But not only did I feel the value of fraternity for its own sake, I was also persuaded (and, of course, am still) that without it there could not be either full liberty or full equality. If this is true, then, at least under the conditions of forty years ago with so few opportunities for the growth of fraternity, there was ground for our risking some painful tensions in pursuing the hope of that deeper mutual understanding and trust between black and white which alone can support and buttress the liberty and equality we also seek.

But what stands out in memory for both Lois and me is not such painful tensions as occasionally were felt, but the warmth of so many happy relationships and the kindness with which we were generally received. Very soon, almost at once, we were quite "color blind." Often when an acquaintance's name was mentioned, we had to think twice to remember whether he was black or white—if indeed, as was rarely the case, there was any occasion for remembering this fact about him at all. In view of the brutal treatment to which the black man had so long and so constantly been subject, we were amazed and filled with admiration in discovering how many Negroes seemed to have escaped, or to have overcome, the permanently wounding effects, whether of the intimidating or the embittering kind, which might have appeared inevitable. We found men and women, scorning alike both obsequiousness and hatred; assuming the good will and fairness of others and accepting it as a matter of course, but at the same time "making no peace with oppression" and accepting without protest no violation of their dignity as persons or of that of their brothers; just and open with others and expecting others to be just and open with them.

Under all the conditions of Negro life in America, what moral achievement could have been greater than this?

Chapter 5

Some Disappointed Hopes

NEAR THE BEGINNING of my account of life at Fisk, in speaking of its critical meaning and effect, I used the words: "... so fully was I committed to being there, so much of what I most deeply believed was involved in my being able to stay there, and so deeply disturbing, therefore, so threatening to some of my dearest values, was the discovery that I could not." It remains for me to tell something of how this discovery came about and to indicate the circumstances of our departure.

Near the end of my fifth year at Fisk, in the spring of 1934, I concluded that since I was working, and had every expectation of continuing to work, in this institution of higher education, I should become as competent as possible in some academic field; and this meant, in practical terms, that I should resume and complete the graduate work at the University of Chicago which had been abruptly broken off some seven years earlier. I applied for a year's leave of absence at Fisk and sought in several quarters the financial assistance which would enable me to take advantage of it. The leave was generously granted, and also my other requests: a scholarship at the University of Chicago, a fellowship from the Council on Religion in Higher Education, and a more substantial grant from the American Missionary Association, the Congregational organization which had founded Fisk (and many other such colleges) and still liberally supported it. The president was able to secure as my substitute at the chapel for the year the Rev. William Faulkner, who had been the pastor of a Congregational church in Atlanta and who had been a friend of mine for several years. When the three of us left Nashville for Chicago in the summer of 1934, I knew with great satisfaction that I was leaving my work in good hands indeed.

I shall be speaking in a different connection of our fifteen months in Chicago. At the moment it is enough to say that it proved to be a very rewarding year in many ways, not the least important of the satisfactions being the receiving of my Ph.D. degree in August of 1935.

During this period at Chicago, however, for all my preoccupation with my work there, I was always very much aware that I was on leave of absence from Fisk University and that my basic and, I thought, my permanent, connection was with that institution. What I was doing was being done to make more efficient and valuable the services I might render there. It will be understood, therefore, how profoundly disturbed I was when early in 1935, about midway of my leave, the president at Fisk wrote to suggest that when I returned the following September I should serve simply as professor of religion and that Mr. Faulkner should keep the position he had accepted—I had understood, on a temporary basis— as chaplain or, as the title then went, "Minister of the Chapel." He asked whether such an arrangement would be satisfactory to me. Knowing me as I think he did, he amazed and deeply pained me by asking such a question. The chapel position and what I thought it implied as to my place in the confidence and affections of the community had been hardly less than my life for five years. What did this suggestion mean? Did it mean that I had been mistaken in thinking that I had filled my position satisfactorily? And if so, did the failure lie in me as a person, a preacher, a pastor—or in me simply as a white man? In either case, the disillusionment would be great indeed.

There was a succession of letters between Dr. Jones and me. Unfortunately for my present purpose I find I do not still have the correspondence; but its general character and content I remember only too well. I answered his original letter (as I feel sure he must have known that I would), expressing my sense of shock at the proposal that I should relinquish my position at Fisk and the great grief I should feel in doing so. I spoke of how much the privilege of being personally related to the members of the Fisk community in the peculiar way a minister is to those he serves—how much this privilege had meant to me. I said that I could well understand the success Mr. Faulkner had apparently had, that I expected it, and that I rejoiced in it. I asked, however, if it might not be possible for the university to use us *both*, as a team. No increase in budget would be involved. I urged that I should enjoy my life at Fisk even more than I had always enjoyed it and should find my work even more meaningful than it had always been if Mr. Faulkner and I could thus share in it. I pointed out that such an arrangement was possible because of the friendship and mutual regard which existed between us and that a partnership of this kind between a black man (for Mr. Faulkner was a Negro) and a white man might be of great significance. In view of the interest of the university in interracial progress and in remaining itself as fully interracial in character as the law would permit, would not such a partnership be peculiarly appropriate there? I pleaded with all the vigor which strong conviction and almost desperate desire could engender, never that I be returned to my sole place as minister, but that I not be entirely shut out of it. But the original "suggestion" had rapidly become a definite requirenent, and even the "part in the action," as I had proposed and urged it, was firmly denied me.

I knew then that my days at Fisk were numbered. I had no interest in being a professor of religion in a college. I had tried this role at Emory and had decided it was not my true one. I was basically a minister, not a professor. I belonged primarily to the church, not to the school. I foresaw that I might possibly eventually teach in a theological seminary, where the necessary relationship of roles might be maintained, but not in a college, where, it seemed to me at least, it could not. But the principal reason for my conclusion that I could not continue at Fisk was the realization of the absence of confidence in me, either on the part of the president or the people (or a significant number of them), which was clearly implied in the president's action. I should not necessarily have drawn this conclusion if the issue had been simply my resuming the role which Mr. Faulkner had temporarily taken. But since all I was asking for was the privilege of being associated with him in the work of the chapel, I could see no meaning in the firm refusal other than a wish to discourage me from continuing longer at Fisk. I knew that in view of the grant which had been made me by the American Missionary Association I was obligated to return for the following year. But I recognized that, unless there was some quite unexpected development, I would probably not remain longer.

After my return to Nashville, I felt helpless to make inquiries, but obviously it was a matter of great concern to me to know whether the disaffection toward me was principally the president's or the people's. I could not doubt that the president would hardly have acted as he did without grounds in the satisfaction of many persons in Mr. Faulkner's presence and service. I knew that if I had been there as a member of the congregation during the year of his "acting chaplaincy" I should have felt the same satisfaction. And it was more than credible to me that many, even a majority, of the people might prefer him to me. If the question had been that of a choice between us, I could believe that this preference, if it existed and was decided enough, might have forced the president's hand in discontinuing my appointment. But I found it hard to believe that either Mr. Faulkner or the community would have rejected my request simply to share with him in the doing of the job which I had been given every reason for thinking was my own. I doubted, and doubt still, that either was consulted about my proposal of a partnership or ever knew that it was made. Neither then nor later did I feel free to inquire.

In other words, although I could easily understand and accept with the most cordial feelings the people's liking for and confidence in Mr. Faulkner, I could not, in the light of all my experience at Fisk, believe that there was a corresponding dislike for and lack of confidence in me. This assurance was of the greatest importance to me in adjusting to what was, in any case, a bitter disappointment. Without it, I should have suffered a very severe loss of confidence indeed, not in myself only—that would have been a relatively unimportant loss—but in the possibility of interracial life of any deep and authentic sort. Under no circumstances, I hasten to add, could I have felt any doubt of this possibility within small circles: I had realized this authentic community in my own experience too surely ever to question it. But was this possibility realizable more generally, or among large numbers? I believed it was (what have we to hope for if it is not?) and that my experience should not be regarded, at any rate by me, as an indication to the contrary. The university's rejection of my proposal of a partnership was not to be understood as our community's rejection of Lois and me, either as persons or as white persons, but rather represented an executive decision.

The president's decision—if I am right in thinking that it was largely his own decision—may, of course, conceivably have been taken on the grounds (I am sure, mistaken) that the plan of shared responsibility would not have worked. But I suspect that it had deeper grounds. He and I did not see eye to eye on several matters of social and educational policy, and particularly on one matter. About this matter there were over several years, as I recall, a few serious conversations—one of these, in the fall of 1934, an almost acrimonious one. And any adequate account of my life at Fisk must contain some reference to this important difference.

Fisk University, as I have said, like most of the other so-called Negro colleges in the South, was established by a church body in the North to serve the desperate needs of the Negro people just after the Civil War. If this kind of action had not been taken and the states had been depended on to provide educational opportunity for the newly emancipated slaves, one cannot say for how many years this opportunity, especially for anything like higher education, would have been denied. It was decades after the founding of such colleges as Fisk, Talladega, Le Moyne, and scores of others, all under church auspices, before the states began to offer any means of higher education to their Negro citizens —or rather, as things were, their Negro subjects.

The original staffs of the private church-related colleges, both in administration and teaching, were almost without exception white men and women, motivated by Christian convictions, in the pre-war period dedicated to freeing the Negro and now dedicated to serving him. These men and women had come into a social situation as alien and often as hostile as any foreign land could be, and they had identified themselves with the Negro absolutely, without reservation or exception. Such identification, desired as it no doubt

was by them, would in any case have been forced on
them by the absolute exclusiveness of the surrounding white
society. When I went to Fisk in 1929, several of these early
"missionaries" were still there. I think of Miss Spence,
Miss Scribner, and a few others. Miss Spence was the eldest
of them, the daughter of one of the band of founders,
herself a teacher in the university for many years, long
since retired, but more truly and deeply a member of the
Fisk community, perhaps, than anyone else there. No one
at Fisk, I believe, would have denied the crucial importance
of what such pioneers had done.

But times had greatly changed. The occasion for the
original mission of these pioneers had long since passed.
The Negro wanted a fair chance to help himself, not
another to help him. The idea of someone's coming to
him as a "missionary" was abhorrent. I could not help feeling, however, the presence among the students at Fisk of
what may at first appear to be a curious ambivalence on
this matter. On the one hand, there was the natural aversion
toward the "missionary," toward any white person who had
come presumably to "help" them. But at the same time, the
most beloved white people on the campus were undoubtedly
the older "missionaries" who were still there. (One of the
first of a series of new buildings was named Scribner Hall.)
The explanation of this apparent discrepancy lies, I think, in
the completeness of the *identification* with themselves which
they felt in such persons as Miss Spence. Simply for reasons
of history, if for no other, these old teachers belonged to
them. And, as I sensed the psychological realities, while
anything remotely resembling *condescension* on a white
person's part was hateful (and condescension was, rightly
or wrongly, associated with the "missionary," at any rate with
any newly arriving "missionary"), a white person's *identification* with them, if they could believe it was real and sin-
cere, was deeply needed and highly valued. We are back

again to the theme touched on earlier that it is not by accident that the French Revolutionary motto was threefold: "liberty, equality, *fraternity.*"

Dr. Jones, the president, was well aware of the aversion to the professional "missionary." As to how far he shared the aversion I do not know; I am sure he thought he shared it altogether. He suffered, however, in some quarters, under the handicap of having been himself a missionary to Japan and of having brought to the faculty several white persons who had been missionaries abroad. It is possible that this fact led him, in reacting against the missionary stereotype, to overreact—that is, to overlook, or to discount, the necessity of that *identification* with the Negro, or the longing for it, of which I have just spoken. The president's theoretical position was that Fisk was a "college"—not a Negro college, but simply a college. Its faculty should be composed of the men and women, white and black indiscriminately, who were most competent to teach their respective subjects, with no regard whatever to any other consideration. If a particular man or woman, happening to be white, were the best person in biology or philosophy for Amherst or Wellesley, he or she was ipso facto the best person in biology or philosophy at Fisk. Obviously, such a person would need to be willing to instruct, and work with, Negro students; he must not have any active or virulent race prejudice. But the race of his Negro students could, and should, be disregarded as entirely incidental and irrelevant, not only in his personal dealings with them—*with respect to that point, needless to say, I entirely agreed*—but also in his *decision* to accept a position where he *would be* dealing with them, and with them almost exclusively.

As I have already indicated, I found myself profoundly disagreeing with this understanding of the appropriate motivation of the white man or woman who decided to join the Fisk University faculty of forty years ago. I had sought to be at Fisk specifically *because* it was an interracial and predominantly Negro community and because I should have there the opportunity of living and working with *Negroes*. The racial character of the community, far from being incidental so far as that choice was concerned, had been the only reason I had made it; at that very moment I might have chosen to go to Antioch. And yet it would have been entirely false to say that I belonged in the "missionary" category, and I do not think that anyone at Fisk thought of me so. The reason why I wanted to be at Fisk, or at such an institution, was not that I wanted to "help Negroes," as though without white help they would be helpless—far, far from it! Rather I wanted the privilege of being personally associated with Negroes, of learning from them and sharing with them, of disassociating myself as far as I could from the dominant racial mores, and of contributing, if possible, to interracial understanding and the achieving of a fully integrated society.

An indication of how this difference of opinion between the president and me could have caused friction, as well as a clearer notion of my own position, will be provided perhaps by an illustration or two. Because I knew that Dr. Jones was well aware of my profound disagreement with him, I was surprised when, happening to be in Chicago, I received a letter from him asking me to visit a certain librarian in that city whom he was trying to interest in the position of librarian at Fisk, which had recently become vacant. The first remark the Chicago librarian, a white man, made to me was in substance this: "Dr. Jones writes me that Fisk University is simply a college in Nashville and that the fact that all the students and at least half of the faculty are Negroes is a fact of no importance, need make no difference in my way of living, and should have no weight in my decision. Would you say that this is true?"

Since, as I have said, Dr. Jones had every reason for knowing what kind of answer I would make to such a question, I felt there was no betrayal of trust involved when I made it. I said that in my opinion the largely Negro constituency of the college *was* a fact of supreme importance for a white person considering a place there; that membership in its faculty, if it were sincerely and appropriately accepted, would involve as much identification with the Negro as was possible for a white person and therefore no small measure of voluntary separation from the white community; that unless a white person accepted a position at Fisk University because it was a Negro college and offered an opportunity for sharing with Negroes in a truly interracial life, he should decline it.

The man replied that he felt as I did about the principle of the thing; and that since he was a librarian and wanted simply to be a librarian, having no particular interest in knowing, or sharing in, the Negro's distinctive experience, he would reject Dr. Jones's offer.

I recall at least one other incident of this kind. It happened after I had left Fisk but does not serve less well on that account to set forth the position I had always held. A young man wrote me to say that he had been invited to accept a teaching post at Fisk University. He knew that I had previously lived and worked there and would like me to tell him what sacrifices one's accepting such a position would require. He said that he inferred from what Dr. Jones had said to him that no sacrifices at all would be entailed, that he himself would be as free of social limitations as if he were teaching at Vanderbilt or any other college. But he found it difficult to believe that this could be true and wished confirmation from me. I answered—though less bluntly perhaps than I shall now say it—that a white person moved to ask the question he had asked was not suited to membership in the Fisk faculty; that no white person on the faculty of such an institution who did not think of its largely black constituency as a decided, indeed the decisive, "plus," and in no sense or degree as a "minus," should be there; that a person, like himself, offered a position there who found himself wondering whether he should accept it *even though* it was a Negro college should, simply in virtue of that fact about himself, reject the offer; that only if he found himself eager to be there just *because* it was an institution of that kind, should he be there at all. How, I asked, could a white person, who if he were academically and personally qualified might find a satisfactory position in many a white college, be justified in taking a place which otherwise would be occupied by a probably equally well-qualified black man or woman, to whom teaching positions were not open except in the few Negro colleges—how could the white man be justified unless he was concerned, not only with teaching his subject, but also with sharing in a truly integrated interracial life, thus incidentally contributing what he could to the healing of the nation's racial wounds? The young man replied sometime later that he agreed with what I had said and that in consequence, he had rejected the offer.

Before my way of justifying a white man's presence in the faculty of Fisk or any similar institution is judged wrong, let it be remembered that I am speaking about a situation of forty years ago. The state of affairs today (in 1973) is very different, and it will become more widely different still with each advancing year. Negroes are now members of college and university faculties throughout the country, south and north. John Hope Franklin, for example, one of my students, is professor of history at the University of Chicago. Florence Beatty Brown, another student friend at Fisk, holds a distinguished position as head of the Division of Social Sciences in Meramec College in St. Louis. These are only two examples of scores which might be cited. Many predominantly white educational institutions are actively seeking qualified Negro teachers and research scholars. Few previously all-white colleges, north and south, are not now open to Negro applicants; and many such colleges are actively soliciting them. Higher education in America is rapidly becoming desegregated.

But this development was hardly as much as a dream forty years ago. That my own alma mater, Emory University in Atlanta, should in 1973 have even a few black students would in 1933 have been quite incredible. One can now foresee the time when such institutions as Fisk, Talladega and Morehouse will be, as Dr. Jones said, "just colleges," along with Williams, Vassar, and William and Mary—all fully and freely interracial. But in the decade of the thirties that time had not even come within sight. Fisk, Talladega, and Morehouse were not "just colleges"; they were colleges of a very special kind. And I shall always maintain that the white person who in those days undertook a place of leadership within one of them needed to have attitudes and motives of a correspondingly very special kind.

On the one hand, such a white person needed to be absolutely color-blind in all his personal relations with his Negro students and colleagues, not so much ignoring the difference in race between himself and them as not being aware of it at all. This would obviously have been the basic element in his special qualification for living in such a community as Fisk University, and it is, just as obviously, the permanently indispensable element. But as things were, there was another requisite which was, then at least, almost equally important. The Fisk community did not exist in a vacuum. It was a part of American, and specifically of southern American, society. And in his relations with that society and in his relations with his Negro students and associates *as members of it,* the qualified white person could not for a moment be color-blind. For that society was not. On the contrary, it distinguished sharply between the white man and the black and discriminated cruelly against the latter. The white man must dissociate himself, as far as was possible for such a man, from this pattern of separation and discrimination; he must identify himself with the Negro, not only as a human being, but also specifically as a Negro, sharing in his deprivations—again as far as a white person could—and joining the Negro in the battle for justice and equality. I have called this combination of color-blindness and clear and poignant color-awareness a qualification of a very special kind. But was it not a manifestly necessary qualification? And indeed until "liberty, equality, fraternity" fully prevail in our society as a whole, will it not always be such for any white person who aspires to belong to, and to serve in any important capacity, a largely black community?

I have said enough, I hope, to make clear the nature of the differences between the president and me, and also their importance. That they had nothing to do with the administrative decision which excluded me from the work I had come to Fisk to do, I find incredible.

At the same time, I was forced to realize that if there had been a sufficiently strong desire on the people's part that I continue in my old position, the president's action in refusing me even a share in it would have been difficult, if not impossible. Not that I had any doubt of the confidence and affection of many of the students and of a number of my colleagues and of many other members of the college community and its neighborhood! How could there have been such doubt in view of all the friendships with which I had been blest through seven years at Fisk, not to mention earlier experiences! But I could not fail to be disappointed that I had not been even more richly blest. My having to leave was therefore a disillusioning as well as a disappointing fact: it revealed how difficult of achievement, even beyond my expectations, my goal had been. For I had been as sincerely devoted to seeking it and had sought it as zealously as, I believe, any person could.

Letting a few outside friends know that I must leave Fisk,

I was invited by Dr. Morrison to join the editorial staff of *The Christian Century* in Chicago and, more specifically, to assist him in launching a new quarterly magazine *Christendom*. We took leave of Nashville in the summer of 1936. I left with great sadness. My hopes, as the hopes of youth so often are, had been too high.

This departure from Fisk University marked the end of any experience I have had of living as a member of a largely Negro community. I went back into the predominantly white world and have lived there ever since. As will have been seen, I went reluctantly. But if it be thought that any "defense" is needed of my return to conditions of life from which I had hoped to be freed, I fear I cannot offer an adequate one. I could say that no similar opportunity of interracial living has ever been offered me. But then I should also have to say that I have not actively sought it. I could also say that Lois and I have been steadfastly unwilling to settle into any place or to enter into any association from which Negroes as such were excluded, and that this has meant until very recently that our life and work have been in the northern states whereas on every other count we should have preferred the area where we were born and nurtured and where we have been offered attractive opportunities of being. But, then, I should need to confess that I might have been more energetically engaged than I have been in protesting and correcting such discrimination. I could say that I have never been fully comfortable even in a situation in which Negroes would have been welcomed, if in fact they were not present in it. But I should have to add that I have not been as vigorous as I should have been in seeking their presence. In a word, I must confess to many sins of omission.

But on the "commission" side, I believe I can truly say,

without any qualification or retraction, that since my Emory days, I have never, either through word or deed or silence, been disloyal to any Negro or to the Negro people and to the principle of equality as to every human right and dignity. Nor have I ever doubted that human relations can be as close and warm across racial lines as within them and may, other things being equal, be even more rewarding. As I have said more than once, many of the friendships with Negroes which we made at Fisk and earlier are still an active and important part of our lives, and many more are treasured in memory—not to speak of the many such friendships formed in subsequent years. From my present vantage point of seventy-two, after my second retirement from active work, I look back upon my five years as Minister of the Chapel at Fisk University as the most significant period in my career.

Chapter 6

Chicago: 1934 - 1943

I HAVE TOLD of my having been granted by Fisk University in
1934 a year's leave of absence for graduate study at the
University of Chicago and of my receiving my doctor's degree in the next summer. But I offered no account of what
happened in that year beyond some developments in my relations with Fisk. Indeed, the period was mentioned only as
an episode in my experience in that institution. Lois and I
thought of it at the time in the context of our Nashville life:
it was the sixth year of however many years we were to
spend at Fisk. But from the point of view of a later time, the
year has a different aspect. As things worked out, we were to
spend only one more academic year at Fisk, and that year
was to be very different from the five exciting and happy
years which had preceded my leave. Besides, at its end, and
after an absence of only nine months, we were to return to
Chicago and were to reside there almost continuously for
another seven years.

It is not strange, then, that Chicago stands in memory as
the principal locus of our life for the whole period 1934–43,
and that instead of its being true that the year for study is
remembered as an interruption of our Nashville life, the final
nine-months term at Fisk appears in memory of an interruption of our Chicago life. To be sure, still another nine-months

interruption was to occur—my brief tenure in 1938–39 of an associate professorship at the Hartford Theological Seminary in Connecticut. But, even so, Chicago clearly dominates the entire period and provides such chronological continuity as it has. I shall attempt some account of all three parts of it— the times when I was a student, when I was an associate of Dr. Morrison in an editorial office, and when, after the short Hartford term, I was for four years a member of the University of Chicago Divinity School faculty.

Going back, then, to my year for study, I take up the thread of this narrative in June of 1934, when Lois, Jack, and I began our residence of fifteen months as a student family in Chicago. We had secured housing for the first summer in the home of a professor on vacation. But during the regular school year and the summer following we lived at three or perhaps four addresses, as we groped for accommodations in the university neighborhood which were both tolerable and priced within the limits of our meager means. It could not have been a very comfortable time, physically at least, but in other respects it was a successful year. The kindness of the Morrisons, of whom I have spoken in connection with my six-months stay at the university seven years earlier and with whom I did not lose touch in the interim, was now extended to the family. We enjoyed the hospitality of the Tafts, and the Paul H. Douglases (the former Emily Taft and her husband) were also warmly friendly. We rejoiced in a growing circle of acquaintances, some of them becoming close friends —Paul Schubert, for example, and Massey Shepherd. Pomp Colwell, my dear old friend from Emory days with whom I had come to Chicago in 1927 was still there. Being more constant than I had been able to be then, he had received his Ph.D. degree in 1930 and, because of his brilliant record and prospects as a scholar, had immediately been made a member of the New Testament faculty. He and his wife Annette were, needless to say, our frequent companions and an unfailing support. I had the privilege of being introduced by Pomp to New Testament textual criticism, in which he was destined to become the acknowledged American authority, and of having his expert guidance and generous help in all my studies.

As I think of the contribution of the University of Chicago to my life, personal and professional, I cannot clearly distinguish between my earlier briefer sojourn there and the longer culminating period in 1934–35, and I shall make no attempt to do so. Just as the university authorities allowed my work in 1927 to count toward my degree, so in their effects in my experience the two periods are merged inseparably. Whatever debt I owed the university in 1935 was a debt I had begun to incur in 1927 and which in a real sense was accumulating in the years between, for the initial six months had continuing and developing influence. I have spoken with loyalty and warm regard of my two previous alma maters—Randolph-Macon and Emory. I have always felt for the Divinity School of a generation ago a special gratitude and affection.

I shall make no attempt to describe the incalculable riches of a personal kind which were poured into my lap during my time there, by friends and by teachers and through classroom and chapel, not to speak of the innumerable less formal occasions for fellowship and mutual helpfulness which were involved in the intimacy and concrete fullness of the common life. I shall also leave largely unspoken my gratitude for certain particular courses which have meant much to me; for example, a course with Professor Henry Nelson Wieman in what was, I believe, his first quarter at the university. Wieman had just written his *Wrestle of Religion with Truth*, and our course was almost entirely devoted to a page-by-

page study of Whitehead's *Religion in the Making*. This was
my introduction to Whitehead as well as to Wieman, and I
remember it as one of the really important experiences of my
life. But there are other memories of this kind, and I cannot
speak separately of them. What I shall try to do is to comment briefly on two rather general and pervasive characteristics of the Divinity School of those days which stand out
in my memory of it and indicate, in large part, the nature
of the debt I owe to it.

The first of these was the overflow of a devoted, enthu-
siastic, and infectious interest in research—an interest
which, so far as I know, had been characteristic of the
institution since the days of Harper and perhaps before,
for the Divinity School antedated the founding of the
university. In New Testament and early church history,
the professors, when I first came in 1927, were Goodspeed,
Case, Votaw, Willoughby, and Riddle. By 1934, Votaw had
dropped out and, as I have said, Colwell had joined the
distinguished group. It did not take the entering student
long to find out that these men could be the good teachers
they were because they were primarily, not teachers at
all, but learners, and that their learning was an effort, not
merely to master old facts, but also to uncover new ones
or—even more important and exciting perhaps—to make the
old ones themselves new by placing them in fresh perspec-
tives and connections. My initial interview with a member
of the New Testament department was with Don Riddle. I
recall that his first remark after we had exchanged our
names was a query about what I was working on. Having
come, as I thought, to be "worked on," I was a bit startled
by the question. But it well represents the assumption our
professors made about us. They were students; they assumed that we also were students. And we were challenged
to become their younger colleagues in a common task fraught
with stirring possibilities.

In those days we were, rightly or wrongly, less occupied than students nowadays have become with questions about the immediate relevance of our studies. I think we were also, falsely or truly, a little more secure in our own inner existence, so that there was a greater readiness to become interested in truth for its own sake and to find the discovery of it exciting, even when in the particular instance it had no obvious use of a practical kind and did not help to solve any pressing problem, whether personal or social. When I first arrived in 1927, Dr. Goodspeed had only recently published his *New Solutions of New Testament Problems,* and when I finished my work at the university in 1935, his *The Meaning of Ephesians* had just appeared. The years between were undoubtedly kindling and rousing for him, for these were the years when his hypothesis about the collection and publication of the letters of Paul was being developed. Whatever the course one was taking with him, one could not fail to sense his enthusiasm for his idea, his confidence in its truth, his vision of its importance. He was literally filled with it to overflowing, and no one could be immune to the contagion of his excitement and his joy.

A story he told us illustrates this characteristic. He and Mrs. Goodspeed had taken a trip to California by car a number of years earlier. They had left their home on Woodlawn Avenue, had stopped at the University of Chicago Press just long enough for him to run in with the manuscript of *The Formation of the New Testament,* which he had finished the night before, and then had headed west across the plains. In this book he had proposed and briefly discussed the idea that Ephesians might have been a general letter written by the collector of the Pauline letters to serve as a "covering" epistle, a kind of preface to the collection. The idea had only just occurred to him, was wonderfully appealing and stimulating, and he was not able to leave it behind with his manuscript. He continued to think about

it all day in the car. Suddenly the question "popped" into his mind whether another "collection" of letters, the letters to the seven churches in the Book of Revelation, did not begin with a general "letter" to them all. Although he had, of course, read Revelation scores of times and had made his brilliant translation of it, he could not remember whether it did or not—he had never read Revelation with that question in his mind. He told how all day he was tantalized by his uncertainty and asked us to imagine his delight when, reaching a room in the hotel at the end of the day, he went at once to the Gideon Bible and found out that his surmise was true. There was something boyish in his enthusiasm, and we ourselves were then young enough to share it.

His exhilaration was particularly infectious in my case because I became very much preoccupied with Dr. Good-speed's general idea and with some of the problems it suggested. Out of this reflection came my small book *Philemon Among the Letters of Paul,* which both rests upon and, I believe, confirms and significantly supplements Dr. Good-speed's hypothesis. The same thing can be said of my later book, *Marcion and the New Testament.*

The second of the two characteristics of the Divinity School of forty years ago which stand out in my memory and for which I am especially grateful was the emphasis upon social process in the understanding of both the history of the church and its theology. I felt at first considerable resistance to this emphasis. In my first formal interview with Dean Shailer Mathews, when I was registering for my first quarter, I recall his urging me very strongly to enroll in the college in a course in social psychology. I was quite obstinate in my unwillingness to do so, not only because, having come to study theology and particularly the New Testament, I did not want to use my time in the way he proposed, but also because I resented a little an assumption often made in those days, among students at least, that Chicago had its own particular and distinctive position and method, its own peculiar theological stance and style, and that students were expected to adopt it. Dr. Mathews did not insist that I take the course, although it is likely that I should have profited from following his counsel.

But this emphasis upon the social was prevalent and pervasive and was subtly, powerfully effective. In our own field of study Professor Goodspeed stood largely aloof from this way of looking at things, from what was called "the social-historical method"; but Professor Case was fully committed to it. It would not be enough to say that he practiced the method; rather, he instinctively and unconsciously exemplified it. It was the natural law of his intellectual life. In my memory of the University of Chicago in my student days, he stands for this aspect of life there just as Dr. Goodspeed symbolizes the other.

Those of us who remember Professor Case as a teacher will not need to be told of his genius for realism, his impatience with abstractions of all kinds, his quick and sure discernment of the human stuff of which every historical event and development were composed. Before the "form critics" had their later vogue, and quite independently of their influence, he was forcing us to look *through* the ancient documents of the New Testament to the ancient life reflected in them and forcing us also to see this life in the most realistic way possible for us.

Sometimes I felt that Dr. Case did not take individuality seriously enough, did not recognize sufficiently the measure of integrity and autonomy an individual man might possess, or sense the peculiar depths in every man's existence which make him distinctively and unconfusedly himself. This fault, if fault it was, had the effect, as I saw it, of leading him on occasion both to discount unduly the importance of the great individual in the history of the church and also to take too dim a view of the moral possibilities of the ordinary man. But one cannot expect of a scholar with as clear and sure a vision as Dr. Case had of a vitally important truth and with as much power as he had to impart it—that he should always keep things in perfect proportion. And there can be no doubt that the truth he emphasized was vitally important: every man belongs to a historical process and his life is in large part determined by it. Even when I left the Divinity School I was only beginning to see what this statement means. And, needless to say, I do not fully see its meaning now. But of its importance I have become constantly more aware, and it has had much to do with the direction my own thinking has taken about the meaning of Christ and the Christian life.

That direction has in some ways perhaps been different from that which Dr. Case would have envisaged. His teaching has helped make me much more of a Catholic than I was in those days—or, at any rate, recognized that I was—and, I suspect, he would hardly have had this expectation about any of his pupils. I do not think I am mistaken in the impression that it was he who in one of his lectures was insisting that we could properly speak of "churches," but not of "the Church." And yet the whole effect of his teaching was to emphasize the concreteness, the distinctiveness, the creativeness of Christianity as an actual human community and, therefore, implicitly at least, its cohesiveness, its solidity, and its unity. I doubt that he saw what powerful support the "social historical method" could be made to bring to a theology which finds the *substance* of Christianity in a "social-historical" movement—namely, in the church—but does not find it less significant or less precious, on that account. He made much of the influence of its environment upon that movement. At the time, our state of mind being what it was, it was this emphasis which probably struck most of us with greatest force. But always implied and often expressed was the recognition on his part of both the autonomy of the movement and its socially transforming power. I am writing this in 1973; I might have written it in 1953 or possibly in 1943; but I could not have written it in 1935, when my student days at the university ended and I returned for a time to Fisk. But it was as true then as later.

When in 1936 we left Nashville the second time for Chicago, although I was disappointed and somewhat disillusioned, a pleasant sense of adventure was not altogether lacking. My work had always been in either a parish or a school; I was now to try a new profession, that of an editor.

The Christian Century, at that time the most influential, and possibly the best, of American religious journals, had been founded by Dr. Morrison. He had years earlier got control of a failing weekly magazine representing the denomination of the Disciples of Christ, to which he belonged as a minister. He had given the magazine a new character, developing it into an interdenominational and theologically liberal weekly which took "the world as its parish," becoming a powerful voice for both ecumenism and the social gospel, and which commanded great respect both within Christian circles and outside.

Dr. Morrison was editor-in-chief, and a capable and brilliant one he was. The cutting edge of the magazine, particularly theologically and as regards church life, was supplied by him. He provided much of the intellectual weight and thrust of the journal. Anyone who had known it over the years could readily discern the difference in strength and quality when, long after my brief term of service with it, age and failing health forced him to remove his hand.

For all his importance, however, I hesitate to say that he was more important than Paul Hutchinson, the managing editor, in whose hands lay the responsibility of "filling the white pages" and getting the magazine to the press and out of it every week. Paul was in his way quite as capable and as brilliant as the man he called "the boss." He was a journalist *par excellence*—far more knowledgeable about the world than Dr. Morrison, far more sensitive in discerning social and political realities and issues, and therefore much sounder in his judgments about them. He had a keen eye for the pertinent news, the clear and direct style, and the flair for striking, biting comment, which characterize the superb journalistic editor. Without Dr. Morrison *The Christian Century* would have been a much less weighty and editorially powerful journal; without Paul it would have been much less lively and widely relevant. Indeed, without Paul (and I know that Dr. Morrison knew this very well), I do not see that there could have been *The Christian Century* at all—surely not the particular *Christian Century* many thousands knew, trusted, and loved.

These two men were assisted by another equally competent, Dr. Winfred E. Garrison, who served as literary editor and as such took responsibility for all book reviewing, but who also contributed a substantial share of the editorials. He was a professor at the University of Chicago but devoted, as I recall, a large part of two days each week to the work of the editorial office. Dr. Garrison, like Dr. Morrison a loyal, even if somewhat "maverick," minister of the Disciples of Christ Church, taught in church history and was thoroughly at home there, but it seemed to me that he knew quite as much about history in general, about literature old and new and in several languages, and about the arts. He was, besides, something of a musician, something of a poet, and an excellent sculptor. Like the two other men, he had the journalist's instincts and skills, and his contribution to the magazine during the many years of his association with it was enormously rich and far more extensive than any "outsider" could have supposed. Editorials, needless to say, are not signed; but so well established was the literary style of the paper, I should have defied anyone to discriminate between Dr. Garrison's writings and Paul's. Dr. Morrison's were more distinctively recognizable perhaps—but this would have been as much because of the difference of subject matter as of style.

I soon got the hang of things in the office on South Dearborn Street. The paper regularly contained two "long" editorials (in summer, one), each running from one and a half to two pages of the magazine, and nine "shorts," paragraph-long editorials, three approximately to a page. There followed in each issue a series of contributed articles, occasionally solicited but usually submitted on the writers' initiative. A number of notable authors on theological or theological-ethical themes and on various more particular socially significant issues regarded *The Christian Century* as the preferred medium of their occasional essays. The most important of these was Reinhold Niebuhr. For a long time he and Dr. Morrison were close friends, and I know that the latter was very proud of his important part, as he thought of it (and indeed with truth), in "discovering" the young Niebuhr and making him very quickly well known. Dr. Morrison stood in the same relation to Henry Nelson Wieman and performed for him a similar service.

As for the editorials in each issue, Dr. Morrison always wrote one of the two long ones. Most of the rest were written by Paul or Dr. Garrison on topics Paul selected. Paul usually assigned to me two, or possibly three, of the "shorts," and very occasionally I was asked to write one of the long editorials. This was a new kind of writing to me and I found it arduous work, particularly at first. I shall always remember two—perhaps there were even three—weeks as the most strenuous of my whole life, so far as the doing of professional work is concerned. They fell fairly early in my first summer with *The Christian Century*. Dr. Morrison and Dr. Garrison were on vacation, and Paul was doing the work with only the assistance some of us on the staff could give him. Suddenly he was stricken with an abdominal malady and emergency surgery was required. The full responsibility for getting out the paper for the next few weeks had fallen on me. The editorial writing was, needless to say, the biggest part of the job. Discovering each week as many as ten topics appropriate for editorial comment was quite as difficult as writing the comments themselves. But somehow I managed to put the weekly issues together, and though they were surely not the most brilliant in the history of that journal, I doubt that many readers were aware of any substantial departure from the norm.

Paul also called on me to assist him in the work of editing contributed material. As an assistant for a year in the department of English composition at Emory during my student days I had had some experience in correcting student compositions, and this experience now stood me in good stead. I hardly need to say that the good writers asked of the editor only a minimum of work, although I recalled, and found true, a remark once made to me by James Weldon Johnson that there was no writer so good that he could not profit from a good editor's assistance. This is true because it is hard indeed for a writer to hear what he writes precisely as another will hear it. But, of course, the editor must be "good." He must be as careful in avoiding gratuitous changes as firm and sure and felicitous in making needed ones. As far as possible his hand must be undiscernible even to the author himself. If he makes a change he must so nicely understand what the writer has meant to say and so nicely say it that the author never supposes the language is not entirely his own. A friend of mine, Professor C. H. Dodd (who died recently) who wrote and published extensively, speaks somewhere of the "incredible stupidity of editors." Surely there are stupid editors, and few writers have not suffered from them. But I venture to say that even so excellent a writer as Professor Dodd would have been surprised to know how much his books and essays owe to intelligent and sensitive editors. For the editor's work, like the housekeeper's, is not noticed at all unless it is poorly done.

But not every writer whose published work is good writing is a good writer. I had not suspected earlier that this was true. I had always supposed that a poor writer's work would be simply rejected by a publisher. I had assumed that what one read in a periodical or book over or under an author's name was, with very few changes, his own work. I was soon undeceived on both points. Both Paul and Dr. Morrison read many submitted articles which were written abominably, with little regard for grammar and with no regard at all for rhetoric, but which, they felt, were trying to say things interesting or important. Such articles were not infrequently turned over to me. To make a writer say with some clarity and coherence all he meant to say and nothing he did not mean to say when he himself has provided only a blurred picture of something going on in his mind—to do this is no easy task. Moreover, one must do it (if it can be done) in such a way as to leave the writer, when he sees his essay in print, satisfied and proud and happily unaware that any substantial changes have been made in his work. I was amazed to discover how many good writers, well-known and widely published scholars and experts, offered their editors such a task and opportunity.

I say "opportunity," for, except for the time involved, I found an assignment of this kind especially attractive, providing me with as fascinating a challenge as a chess problem must provide a chess expert. In the chess game one tries to understand the intention of another in order to thwart it;

here one is trying to understand that intention in order to forward it. But a poor writer can do a better job in concealing his intention than even the best chess player!

Since those days in *The Christian Century* office, I have been involved in many editorial undertakings. All of them I accepted the more willingly and carried through with greater success because of the pleasure I have always found in trying to puzzle out, and straighten out, the intricate verbal tangles in which, occasionally at least, all but the very best writers get themselves involved. That in this humble occupation I have developed some skill appears, I think, in the fact that although over the years I have copy-edited at least a thousand manuscripts, perhaps as many as twenty-five of book length, I can recall only one protest from an author about an editorial change. Of course, it is possible, and even likely, that there have been objections which were not voiced. But since in most cases the author had the opportunity of making his protest when he read his proofs, I conclude that such unnoted objections could hardly have been very strong or serious. However that may be, among the few kinds of work which it has fallen to my lot to do in the world and which I feel I have done well is the extraordinarily important and extraordinarily nice work of the copy editor, lowly and ordinary as it is commonly thought of as being.

Experience in the South Dearborn Street office provided an unusually good opportunity for initiation into editorial work because of the variety of its activity. Not only was *The Christian Century,* a weekly, published there but, as I have said, a new quarterly theological journal, *Christendom,* was just getting under way. Moreover, Dr. Morrison had ventured into the book publishing field under the name of Willett, Clark and Company, and I was often asked to perform some service in connection with a book manuscript. For *Christendom* I was given—under his oversight and, on all matters of policy, his guiding hand—full responsibility as managing editor. As its name suggests, the journal was based on the presupposition of the reality, the importance, and the catholic (in the sense of the ecumenical and historical) character of the church. Articles were for the greater part solicited, and here I depended (except for writers of book reviews) almost entirely on the imaginative initiative of Dr. Morrison. In the handling of the articles, in the shaping up of each issue and seeing it through the press, I followed procedures now familiar to me from my work with *The Christian Century*, which actually occupied much more of my time than the quarterly could. *Christendom*, I believe everyone would have agreed, was an excellent magazine. But Dr. Morrison before my time in the office ended had concluded that *The Christian Century* enterprise had overextended itself. He gave *Christendom* to the World Council of Churches, under whose auspices it continued to be published for a few years more, and sold Douglas's *Magnificent Obsession*, the one book which had made money for Willett, Clark and Company, to Houghton Mifflin. Later he sold the other books to Harper and Brothers, including two of my own, *The Man Christ Jesus* and *Christ the Lord*.

In the spring of 1938 I was invited to become associate professor of New Testament at the Hartford Theological Seminary in Connecticut. Feeling assured by this time that my future work lay in the field of theological education, I accepted the offer. Both my family and I entered a delightful situation. I found my work significant and congenial. We were comfortably housed on the seminary campus; our relations with my colleagues (especially with my dear friend, Alexander Purdy) and their families were all that could be wished; and we made many student friendships, some of which have remained active over the years since. But we were in Hartford for only a single year. Pomp Colwell had become dean of the Divinity School in Chicago, and I found an invitation to become associate professor of preaching in that faculty and editor of *The Journal of Religion,* which the University Press published, too attractive to be resisted. We returned to Chicago in the summer of 1939.

The story of the final segment of our Chicago life, although it was longer than either of the others, will be more quickly told. I was now settled into my career as a seminary professor. My work was 'much of a piece with the work I was thenceforth to be doing, and any comments on its character and significance which it may occur to me to make can, perhaps, be made more appropriately in later connections. I began by teaching only homiletics, the successor to that notable and able preacher, Charles Gilkey, a friend already and an even closer one in the years to come. But gradually I was permitted to assist in New Testament teaching, and in the final year of my four on the Divinity School faculty, I was professor of preaching and New Testament. Having lived in Chicago for the greater part of five years before this final return, and always, except for a few months, in the university neighborhood, we felt very much at home in our surroundings and had many warm friends. The Divinity School was what it had been when I was a student there— one of the most stimulating and creative spots in America for graduate work in the various fields of theological study— and one could not be there without feeling the exhilaration, even excitement, of the place. To work under Pomp Colwell's leadership was a joy, and relations with other colleagues in the faculty and with students were pleasant and rewarding.

I found the editorship of *The Journal of Religion* particularly congenial. It was now my responsibility, not only to work with manuscripts and see them through the press as I had done with *Christendom,* but also to choose authors and to plan issues. The University of Chicago Press, which published this and many other scholarly journals, was very cooperative; Pomp gave strong support; and a somewhat increased budget made possible some promising initiatives. I am not the proper one to judge how well the editorial work was done during the years, 1939–43; but I confess to having felt some pride when, the post of editor of the University of Chicago Press becoming vacant, I was asked to consider accepting it. It was obviously an important academic position, and I was tempted by it. But, on reflection, I realized that my commitment to being a minister of the church was too deep to permit of my taking so "secular" a job.

It was this same commitment, or sense of calling, which eventually led to my leaving the Divinity School itself. Massey Shepherd, who was one of my faculty colleagues when I first returned, to whom I was especially drawn and who shared with me in many more positive concerns, shared also in this: a dissatisfaction with what was felt by us to be the Divinity School's "distance" from the church. We were reluctant to confess this dissatisfaction with the institution and community which we both loved, either to ourselves or to each other. But it was there and was occasionally voiced. Our school was more aware of itself as being a part of the university than as belonging to the church. Perhaps such a state of things is normal and to be expected in a school of religion within a secular university. But it suited neither Massey nor me. He left in 1940 to be ordained in the Episcopal Church and to accept a teaching position in the Episcopal Theological School in Cambridge, Massachusetts. My own departure was to occur three years later. I did not move, as he did, to a church-related seminary. That was to happen in my case only many years later. But I did turn to an institution which, though closely related to a university, was in most respects independent of it, and though not officially connected with any denomination was, at that time at least, not only primarily committed to serving the church, but also deeply aware of itself as belonging to it. It was not easy to leave Chicago, and particularly the Divinity School. Lois and I struggled long over the issue. But the final, and I think inevitable, decision was to accept the invitation to be professor of New Testament at the Union Theological Seminary in New York, and in the summer of 1943 we made our move.

Before ending this account of our Chicago life, I feel that I want to say at least a little more about Dr. Morrison and my relations with him. He comes closer perhaps than any other single person to binding my Chicago experiences together. I knew him and had begun to love him even before my earliest student days there in 1927. He and his family provided a "home" for me during that period. There was correspondence with him, and an occasional visit, during the time of my residence in Nashville. We were frequently together—and his family and mine—during the year of study in 1934–35. He knew of the distress I felt about the change in my position at Fisk. He generously invited me to return to Chicago in 1936 as an assistant of his own, and my opportunities for association with him became almost constant. And this association continued—though, of course, with less frequent contacts— during the time of my membership in the Divinity School faculty.

I said earlier that Dr. Case had helped make a Catholic of me. This could much more aptly be said of Dr. Morrison, for he was himself in a very true sense a Catholic churchman. Of his several important books, the most important was undoubtedly *What is Christianity?*, which was written during the period of my association with him. He often discussed with me various points as they arose in his work on it, seeking my judgment on them in a way which both humbled and flattered me, and he sometimes deferred to my opinions. We did not always agree; but I felt the appeal of his thesis and the strength of his arguments. It was he, I am sure, who was primarily responsible for my being invited, years later, to give the Hoover Lectures at the University of Chicago, and I dedicated the published lectures, *The Early Church and the Coming Great Church*, to him, using the words of Paul about a friend of his own: "a helper of many, and of me." Such he was, and as such I shall always gratefully remember him.

Chapter 7

The Years at Union: 1943 - 1966

MY YEARS AT the Union Theological Seminary in New York were the most settled, the most active, and in some ways the most productive of my life, and I am somewhat at a loss to know how best to go about giving an account of them. A straight chronological record would be both difficult to write and dull to read. I am inclined to think it may be best to treat of my experience there with attention to various aspects or characteristics of it rather than to the periods into which it might be thought of as falling. And perhaps I cannot do better than to start with the three terms I have just employed: "most settled," "most active," and "most productive."

The first two of these adjectives I use without any hesitation as being obvious factual descriptions. The third I stumble over a bit, not only because of the element of presumption there may seem to be in it, but also because it does not say quite what I mean. In speaking of "productiveness" I am thinking, not of "achievements" or overt accomplishments, if there were any such, but of a certain maturation which took place in these Union years, especially in my theological thinking. The problem of authority in the Christian life, which had always troubled me, came as near to being solved for me as it was ever to be. The same can be said of the more particular question of the relation of Christian faith to history. Other theological gropings attained whatever goals they were destined ever to reach—at a few points at least I came to rest—and, in any case, the *directions* of my searchings were established with some finality. It will be to this more inward history that I shall want to give largest attention. But something must also be said about our situation and circumstances during this period and about the activities in which I found myself engaged.

I have said that these twenty-three years were the most settled of my life. In the ordinary sense, this is perhaps too obvious to need saying. I lived in New York, and indeed at 99 Claremont Avenue, much longer than I have lived anywhere else. This was not quite the case with Lois, whose home had been Atlanta until our marriage, when she was twenty-five. But my meaning in saying "most settled" is not the obvious one, and in the intended sense the statement is as true for her as for me. I mean "most settled" in our *minds*.

When we went to Union in 1943 it was the feeling of us both that we were making our final move before retirement, and this feeling was confirmed from the beginning of our stay there. I must have felt something of the same kind of assurance when we returned to Chicago from Hartford in 1939; at any rate, I can recall saying in those days that I had given Pomp his first job (back in 1924 or '25 at Emory) and that he had given me my last one. But things did not work out so. As I have already told, a vital element in the environment I needed was absent; and the principal reason for my accepting Union's invitation was that I had reason to believe that as a Christian I could more freely and deeply breathe there. The ground for this expectation lay, not only in the reputation of Union as an institution interested primarily in educating ministers for parish work rather than in being simply a graduate school of religion (although it was certainly that, too!), but also in my acquaintance with Henry

Sloane Coffin the president, with Frederick Grant, the professor of New Testament, and, more closely, with Reinhold Niebuhr, Paul Tillich, and Henry Pitney Van Dusen. These three Union men were members of a theological discussion group, which met semi-annually—then at Yale and later at the Episcopal Cathedral in Washington—and which I had earlier been asked to join. This group, over the years, meant much indeed to me, more than I have probably ever recognized, and deserves more than passing reference in this account.

The group had been initiated some five or six years before I became a member in 1938 among some twenty-five of the younger theological scholars. (They were known as the "Younger Theologians" till that name became only too obviously inappropriate.) The original proposal and invitation which had called the group into being expressed the hope that "by full, frank, and leisurely exchange of ideas . . . the thought of all the participants will be greatly fructified," and that "united in a common vital concern for the Christian cause in our day, [they] will be found to share a large body of common convictions—probably larger than any of them now realizes and richer than any of them has been able by himself to articulate." The group had begun its work at a time when, to use the words of Henry Van Dusen written in 1943, "religious thought, even within the Churches, was chaotic . . . 'Naturalistic Humanism' . . . had already spent its strength and, except in limited circles, was no longer a challenge to Christian faith. But . . . an aftermath of scepticism, relativism, and uncertainty . . . was widespread. On the other hand, powerful counter-currents had set in summoning men to a 'return to orthodoxy.'" Discussions over twenty-five years or so explored a wide range of theological issues, and with enriching effect, not only for the participants, but also, I believe, for the church.

One cannot fail to realize, however, as one reads Dr. Van Dusen's words thirty years later, that the state of "thought, even within the Churches" is still "chaotic," that "Naturalistic Humanism" had by no means "spent its strength," and that "scepticism, relativism, and uncertainty" are, if anything, more "widespread" now than then. But of this current situation something will be said later.

Besides the three whose names I have mentioned, some of the more faithful attendants and articulate discussants during the twenty years during which I was an active member of this group were Edwin Aubrey, John Bennett, Seelye Bixler, Robert Calhoun, Samuel Cavert, Virginia Corwin, Angus Dun, Georgia Harkness, Walter Horton, Theodore Greene, John Mackay, Benjamin Mays, Francis Miller, John Moore, James Muilenburg, Stuart Nelson, Richard Niebuhr, Wilhelm Pauck, Douglas Steere, George Thomas, Theodore Wedel, Amos Wilder and Alexander Zabriskie.

I do not need to say that association and growing friendship and understanding with such men and women as these was an incalculably rewarding experience, confirming, deepening and broadening for me the meaning of the church's life, and often clarifying, often correcting, my thoughts about it. Three of them were at Union before I was invited to join them there, and I had already come to know and highly esteem them.

Union had been established by Presbyterians, but from the beginning had been interdenominational in both student body and faculty. Being interdenominational, however, had not meant, as it often does, being separated from all the denominations and therefore, as things unfortunately are, from the church itself as an actual institutional reality. In the spring of 1943, after I had made my decision to go to Union, I had a kind letter from Fred Grant in which, among other things, he said:

"I know exactly how you feel about leaving your friends in Chicago. . . . But I can promise you many warm and growing friendships here . . . not as a substitute for the old because, thank God, they continue, but as a supplement. . . . If you teach here at Union, you belong to all the Church, in an even deeper sense, I think, than is true in any other school. . . . I really think we have the best that all the churches can contribute. I don't mean simply in students, and certainly not in faculty, but in thought, interest, devotion, and enthusiasm. . . . Bishop Tucker, the new President of the Federal Council of Churches, a Virginian, an Episcopalian . . . said to a group of students at my home not long ago: 'As I go about the Church I find that the men who come from Union Seminary are better fitted to preach the gospel and do the Church's work . . . than men from any other Seminary—bar none.' If we are ever to have Church unity, which some of us would gladly give our lives to bring about, it has got to be by the pooling of assets, not by the slow, stingy, paring-down of differences. In that endeavor Union Seminary is not only prophetic but deserves a high part of responsibility in the actual achieving of the dream. I am so glad you are coming to have a share in it."

And I did come, not only to have a share in the unifying of the church, but also to make whatever contribution I could to the enriching and deepening of its life (which is the only way of really unifying it); and the Union of those days offered me every opportunity and encouragment to do so. Common daily worship in the beautiful James Chapel was, particularly in my early years at Union, a vital experience in the life of the whole community. But, more significantly perhaps for me, I could permit a lecture to include a confession of faith or of personal need, or could pray with my students in class or in their rooms without feeling that I was violating the ethos of the community's life or being thought guilty of putting intellectual integrity in jeopardy.

Union had had a long history of distinguished service to the church—a record not to be paralleled in any other institution, if the number of its alumni in places of leadership in the several denominations and in ecumenical church life can be taken as a true criterion. These alumni were doing their work, not alone in this country, but around the world. The seminary had for decades been encouraging, and with generous fellowships enabling, overseas students to come for study. Search committees, most of their members alumni, existed in many lands—in Scotland, in England, in Continental Europe, the Near East, the Far East, Africa, and elsewhere. Their task was to receive applications and to recommend to the seminary the most promising candidates. This policy had enabled the institution to perform a uniquely important service to the church and, incidentally, had enormously enhanced and extended its own reputation.

The great majority of our students were, as I have already hinted, men and women seeking preparation for actual parish work, whether as ministers, directors of religious education, or musicians (for a School of Sacred Music had become a very important part of the institutional life). But always —or at any rate for a very long time—there had been a significant number of graduate students, men and women who had already taken their professional degrees in divinity and who wished to work further in some theological field, usually with a view to teaching in college or seminary. The seminary offered its own master's and doctor's degrees (the S.T.M. and the Th.D.) and also functioned, in effect, as the divinity school of Columbia University, just across the street from us, where several programs leading to the M.A. and the Ph.D. degrees in religion could be pursued.

Union, along with Chicago, Harvard and Yale, was preparing most of the teachers in American seminaries and college departments of religion; and work with the students who looked forward to such a career was one of the most stimulating parts of a Union professor's life.

The faculty was a distinguished one. I have spoken of Reinhold Niebuhr, of Paul Tillich, of Henry Pitney Van Dusen, of Frederick Grant, and of Henry Sloane Coffin. The names of Harry Emerson Fosdick, Russell Bowie, Harrison Elliott, Julius Bewer, Arthur Swift, David Roberts, Cyril Richardson, and Samuel Terrien were among others which could be added to the list of faculty members when I joined it in 1943. John Bennett came at the same time, and we were installed together. Soon afterward John McNeill was to arrive, as I had done, from Chicago, and James Muilenburg, like John Bennett, from the Pacific School of Religion. A little later, Wilhelm Pauck and Daniel D. Williams from Chicago were to join us. Others to come during my term at Union were Mary Lyman, Robert Handy, W. D. Davies, Paul Scherer, Paul Lehmann, John Macquarrie—but I must not even appear to be trying to name all the men and women whose time on Union's faculty coincided with or overlapped my own, not to speak of the many scholars from abroad who served from time to time as visiting professors, such men as John and Don Baillie, T. W. Manson, and C. H. Dodd. I feel fortunate to have served mostly under the presidency of Henry Van Dusen, a most vigorous and enterprising leader and an important theologian with rare administrative and pastoral gifts, during whose incumbency the seminary enjoyed the greatest expansion in its history in physical facilities, size of faculty and student body, and range of educational program. But I am glad also that I was able to be there during the last two years of Dr. Coffin's term and that I saw the beginning at least of John Bennett's presidency. I should be surprised if it does not prove to be true that Lois and I had the privilege of being at Union during the most significant period of that great institution's history.

Of the faculty I joined in 1943 Reinhold Niebuhr and Paul Tillich were undoubtedly the most influential members, both within the walls of the institution and in the intellectual community outside. And I should say that this was true thoughout the whole period of their Union Seminary careers, which were to end in the late 1950s.

Niebuhr I had known to some degree for a long time. He was always in great demand as a speaker to students, and I had first heard him in 1925 at an inter-campus conference at Evanston when I was still a student at Emory. While I was at Fisk, he had been the guest preacher at several of the Sunday services. In Chicago it was not unusual for Dr. Morrison to have him at home for the Sunday evening after his annual sermon in the university chapel, and I had been invited several times for these occasions. The meetings of the "Younger Theologians" had brought me more regularly into touch with him.

There would be no point in my speaking here of the originality and brilliance of his mind, of the breadth of his learning, and of his growing influence, not only among theologians and churchmen generally, but also among political economists and historians—and indeed among politicians, too, for he was very active from the beginning of his career as a pastor in Detroit in the actual implementation of his ethical ideas. All of this is too well known to need any explication here. I never knew a more dynamic personality. As a preacher and lecturer he was superb. He always had something striking and significant to say, and he knew both how to say it and how to stop when it had been said. He spoke without manuscript or notes, but always coherently, incisively, and obviously on the basis of the most careful preparation. He spoke with great vigor; his whole energy, physical as well as mental, seemed to be involved. The more tragic, therefore, was the moment when in the midst of a lecture at Union a stroke suddenly reduced his body to weakness and deprived a still brilliant and active mind of its eloquent voice.

Before this catastrophe he was engaged almost every weekend in some speaking or conference engagement, and I know that many outside the seminary wondered how he could be giving much attention to his intramural tasks. But such persons underestimated both his energy and his conscience. His courses, of which he carried his full load, always had first claim on his time, and he rarely, if ever, missed a class appointment. He was, contrary to the impression of some who knew him only as a public speaker, a most gentle, humble and loving man. I treasure several affectionate letters from him written to me, or to Lois and me, in times of stress in our lives. His students greatly loved him. For many—as many as could be crowded on chairs and floor into the Niebuhrs' large living room—their "at homes" were the high point of every week. I can hardly imagine the Union of those days without "Reinie."

Paul Tillich, who was at Union when I arrived and remained there until his enforced retirement at sixty-nine, was in most obvious ways quite different. I shall not speak of him as a theologian, except to acknowledge thankfully his manifest greatness. His manner of speaking was as far as could be from Niebuhr's—with the voice only, and always quietly, slowly, deliberately. And yet one could not fail to listen to him even when, or if, one could not fully understand him. One could always understand enough to know that something profoundly true and significant was being said, and one's own thought was stimulated by the effort to understand completely. At any rate, this was my experience often in hearing, or conversing with, Tillich, and I cannot but assume it was frequently true of his students also. He, too, was a very gentle man—less outgoing and open than Niebuhr, but amiable and kind. He was charming for many reasons—not least, for a certain naïveté which characterized him. He felt no embarrassment whatever in speaking of "my system," and did so in the most matter-of-fact way, with no suggestion of arrogance. And he was moved, as simply and innocently as a boy might be, by any praise from even the humblest source of what he had said or written. Like Niebuhr's, his contribution to the theology of our own and later generations, needless to say, has been enormous; but his contribution to the life and thought of Union Seminary is also beyond any measurement.

One of the most attractive features of Union was the amplitude of its residential quarters—sufficient to care for both students and faculty in the same complex of buildings. These quarters had at times been strained by increases in both categories; but these stringencies had been repaired, and the policy of making it possible for all members of the community to "live in" was maintained. When Lois, Jack and I went to New York in 1943, we moved into a spacious, eight-room apartment in McGiffert Hall, located in the same city square with the Riverside Church, at 122nd Street and Claremont Avenue. Our windows looked out over the International House gardens and far up the Hudson. These were quarters far more elegant and comfortable than any we had ever occupied before (or, for that matter, have lived in since); and there were the added advantages of our being only across the street (with a connecting tunnel) from the chapel, offices, classrooms and other residence buildings of the seminary and of having as our neighbors other members of the seminary community. When before our leaving Chicago I had spoken of this compactness to one of my friends there, he had expressed his horror at the prospect of our living every day, and twenty-four hours a day, in such contiguity with my work and my fellow workers. But actually he was greatly mistaken. Life in New York is so busy and the centrifugal forces are so strong that, far from having our privacy in any way invaded or impaired, we saw less of our neighbors than we should have liked.

We had been at Union three years and Jack was fourteen years old when our Tony was born—a long and eagerly hoped for event! For still another twenty years the apartment 501 in McGiffert Hall, provided by the seminary as a perquisite, was to be our very secure, commodious, and happy family home.

Six times during this period I was approached about positions in other seminaries. By only one of these was I seriously tempted. When Lynn Harold Hough retired as dean of the Drew Theological Seminary in 1947, I was invited to succeed him. The invitation greatly appealed both to Lois and to me. It offered an exceptional opportunity for service; it represented what might appear to be a "promotion"; and it provided a delightful living situation in the "Dean's House" on the beautiful, wooded Drew campus in Madison, New Jersey, one of New York's quietest, loveliest suburbs. We struggled with the issue, as it seems to me now, for months, having many conversations with Drew's president and others there, and making trip after trip to Madison. In the end, however, I had to decline the generous offer. I did so, not only because of a strong disinclination to leave Union, but also (and decisively) because Drew was a seminary of the Methodist Church, and despite my efforts to convince myself otherwise, I was finally forced to realize that I could never again be so loyal a Methodist as the dean of this seminary should be.

After this episode of indecision, fairly soon after our going to New York, I never seriously considered leaving Union.

Our life there was as near to being "settled" as a teacher's life anywhere or under any conditions can well be.

I have spoken of the years at Union as being also my most active years. When I first came, I was simply a sharer with Dr. Grant in the work of the New Testament department and, because the Second World War was still going on and our student body was abnormally small, that work was not heavy. But this situation was to change abruptly with the war's end and a great influx of discharged servicemen, many of whom had been called to the ministry through their war experiences. Dr. Grant and I found ourselves inundated, and an additional person had to be added to our departmental staff, as was the case also in most of the departments. I shall not try to name all the young men who came to us in this capacity; I think especially of Burton Throckmorton, Christiann Beker, and Louis Martyn—all of them now occupying important positions in various seminaries, Louis being still at Union in the chair Dr. Grant had occupied.

Shortly after my joining the faculty I was given administrative responsibilities which eventually seemed to me to demand more of my time even than my teaching and the immediately needed preparation for it. Dr. Harold Tryon had for many years been serving as registrar of the seminary. But the term "registrar" does not begin to convey the range of services he had been performing. He had been in effect the academic dean, presiding over admissions, students' programs of study, curricular changes, and all similar matters, within very general guidelines. His retirement left an important vacancy—and just at the time when the enrollment of the seminary was rapidly rising. Dr. Grant and I were asked to take over his duties beyond those belonging more strictly

and properly to the registrar's office—Dr. Grant assuming
the responsibility as regards Th.D. and Ph.D. candidates,
and I, as regards the rest of the students (except for those in
the Music School). This office as Director of Studies, much
more important and much more burdensome than, I believe,
the president and faculty of the period recognized it as
being, soon occupied a very significant amount of my attention and time, and a slight reduction in my teaching load
did not begin to compensate for it.

About this time, in 1945 or '46, I became involved in
another activity of considerable importance. Dr. George
Buttrick, then the minister of the Madison Avenue Presbyterian Church, had interested the Abingdon Press in undertaking a biblical commentary series which should represent
the combined work of biblical scholars and expository
preachers. I was asked to join with my colleagues Samuel
Terrien, Russell Bowie, and Paul Scherer, as associate editors, and with Dr. Buttrick himself, as editor-in-chief, in
its preparation. The commentary, which was to run to
twelve volumes, would be called *The Interpreter's Bible.*
An office was set up in the neighborhood of the seminary,
with Miss Elizabeth Stouffer in charge, and all the enormous
editorial work involved was done either there or in the several editors' homes or offices. The project was virtually
completed by 1952, so far as the editors were concerned,
although the last of the twelve volumes did not appear till
1957. The work, from the publisher's point of view, was
a prodigious success. While its publication was still in
progress, the Abingdon Press, again at Dr. Buttrick's suggestion, decided to undertake a large-scale biblical dictionary,
The Interpreter's Dictionary of the Bible, and for four or
five years Dr. Buttrick, Sam Terrien, Herbert May, Thomas
Kepler, and I were engaged in similar fashion in planning
and producing that four-volume work.

During the whole period of my professorship at Union I

was writing in the early morning hours—hours which for forty years or more I have never been able to use in any other way, whether at home or away or in travel. Most of the writing was done in preparation for series of lectures I was from time to time invited to give or in fulfillment of other definite writing or speaking engagements. Nearly all of this writing was, in one form or another, eventually published. Disregarding the unpublished pieces like sermons and some occasional lectures and also short published things like book reviews or notes for encyclopedias or dictionaries, I count twenty-four essays, published either as articles in journals and reference works or as part of various symposia, and nineteen books of various lengths (but none of them very long)—all written during these Union years.

This writing seemed to me the most important of my activities, even though it occupied only the time before morning chapel at 8:30. Whatever its relative importance may really be, it was certainly the most agreeable and satisfying. I did in those early morning hours no reading or research. Such preparation of this kind as I felt was needed for the next day's or any future writing was done at later hours in the day. The habit became so firmly established that, even now, I cannot bring myself to do anything at the beginning of the day after my too-brief prayers but write, even though it be only a letter to a friend. This reference to prayers is not gratuitous because, after my principal interest in New Testament studies turned to the understanding of the religious experience of the early church and to the theological terms in which it was expressed—and this had begun to happen even before my coming to Union— my writing tended to become continuous with my praying and, it might almost be said, a part of it. For once the Christian historian begins to talk about the inner existence of the primitive church, he is considering, not a life belonging simply to the past which can be examined and described objectively or from the outside, but rather his own life as well, or rather a life in which he himself shares. Not only is his own personal existence inseparable from his historical work, but that work could not be truly done if such a separation were imposed. For how can he know truly or adequately a life in which he does not share? And how can he convey its nature without depending as much upon his own experience as upon the records of the experience of others?

There are, needless to say, purely historical questions—I mean questions as to facts belonging exclusively to the past—in answering which one must try strictly to exclude everything but the pertinent objective data. In most of my early work and in some of the later, I have dealt with such questions as faithfully as I could, although, I know, I often did not succeed in being as unbiased and as accurate as I wanted to be. But as the years passed, I found such questions less and less interesting and engaging. As this development occurred and my attention became more and more centered on the life of the early church and on the New Testament as expressive of that life, my own experience as a man and a Christian became increasingly involved.

I am sometimes asked by persons who have been told that I have written some books whether I have ever done any "creative writing." I find this an embarrassing question. To be sure, it is not difficult to say that I have never written poetry or drama or fiction or anything which could presume to belong to the category of belles-lettres. But I am unwilling to allow the phrase "creative writing" to be so narrowly defined. And if I were being entirely frank, I should have to say to the questioner that I thought of most of my writing as being "creative," meaning that it has never been mechanically ground out or laboriously constructed, that it has been a free expression of myself, and that I have done it with a sense of fulfillment. Whether what I have done has been creative for others, I am not the one to say; it has been creative for me. There were times during the period of our New York residence when I should have found it impossible to carry on at all if it had not been for these early morning experiences of freedom and joy.

In the spring of 1957 a rather serious attack of angina forced me to reduce somewhat my working schedule, but I remained busy. The *Dictionary of the Bible* pretty well filled the time left free by the completion of *The Interpreter's Bible*. It is true that I gave up my job as director of studies and that I ceased working in New York during the summers as I had always done before. Furthermore, while continuing to give series of lectures on university or seminary foundations, I virtually ceased going out of the city for occasional addresses and sermons. But new opportunities or duties near at home prevented much slackening of pressure on my energy and time.

Of one of these new opportunities, belonging to the last few years of my life at Union, I must not fail to speak. I had been since 1960 a member of the Standard Bible Committee, the body which had earlier created the Revised Standard Version and now had oversight of it and responsibility for any changes to be made in it. During my period of service on the committee the work involved for me was highly interesting but not very demanding. But in 1964 I received a visit from Monsignor Myles Bourke, the Dean of the Roman Catholic Seminary of St. Joseph in Yonkers and one of the editors of the biblical translation being sponsored by the Bishops' Committee of the Confraternity of Christian Doctrine for use in the mass, who invited me to have a much more significant part in that translation than I could have had in the already completed work of the Revised Standard Version. I was asked to become one of the associate editors and translators of this important project, which was destined to be published in 1970 as *The New American Bible*.

I cannot express how deeply affected I was by this invita-

132 NEVER FAR FROM HOME

tion. My own sense of alienation from my Roman Catholic brethren had long been a source of great grief to me. And when the doors were opened by Pope John and the Second Vatican Council to possible fellowship between Roman and non-Roman Christians, I had experienced what might almost be called a new birth. The first actual sign of the new situation, as far as my own experience was concerned, was a letter from Mother Brady, the professor of Bible at Manhattanville College, the Sacred Heart college for women at Purchase, New York, inviting me to address one of her classes. Needless to say, I accepted eagerly, and Lois and I both spent a happy day with her and other nuns and their students. (There was more than the one such visit before we left New York.)

Some time after this experience I went to Cambridge, to participate in a Harvard University colloquium of Roman Catholic and other theological scholars in celebration of Archbishop Bea's visit to this country. Later still, I was invited to lecture at Notre Dame University during a similar colloquium. On each of these occasions—and there were others—the circle of my Roman Catholic friends was enlarged and my feeling for the reality and catholicity of the church was quickened and deepened. But none of these experiences was so satisfying and rewarding to me as the privilege of preparing translations of several New Testament books and of working one day a week through a large part of a year as a member of a subcommittee with Monsignor Bourke and Father Richard Kugelman C.P. in the editing of these and a number of translations submitted by others.

I have said enough to indicate that my years in New York were far from being idle ones. I should add, perhaps, that I do not think I was more constantly engaged than others of my colleagues.

Something must be told, if this record is to be even summarily complete, about my times of relative leisure during these twenty-three years—for there were such times. I have said that after 1956 I gave up working in the seminary in summers. Lois and I bought an old house and the abandoned farm of about 125 acres in which it stood, and became regular summer residents of Rowe, Massachusetts, a very small rural village in the Berkshires, a mile or two south of the Vermont border. We were just north of what is known as the Mohawk Trail, close to the Deerfield River, about equidistant from Williamstown and Greenfield. The house, built in or around 1780, had been to a considerable degree restored and renovated by the previous owner. With 1958 we began spending our summers there, enjoying the beauty, the quietness, the opportunities for family planning and working (for Tony was always with us, and often Jack) which were provided by the still unfinished house and by the big barn, on which no labor at all had been bestowed for many decades. The fields and woods on all sides, besides surprising us constantly with new nooks and vistas of loveliness, invited us to undertake all kinds of projects to "improve" them. These were happy summers, and it was with a very sharp pang that, when I retired at Union in 1966, we realized that for a variety of reasons we needed to give up the only place we had ever come to love as our very own.

Besides these eight summers of comparative leisure, there were the three sabbatical leaves generously granted me by Union. The first of these, in 1952–53, came after the finishing of most of my work on *The Interpreter's Bible* and before the *Dictionary* had been undertaken. I had been invited by the divinity faculty of Cambridge University to become a lecturer there and had received a Fulbright teaching fellowship to make this possible. At this time Jack was finishing his junior year at Emory University and Tony was about six years old, ready to begin his schooling. The three of us at home did not wish to go without Jack; and he was fortunately able to arrange both with Emory and with his draft board to spend the pre-Christmas term of his senior year at

Cambridge. So the four of us sailed together on the *Media*, spent perhaps a month in travel on the Continent, and settled into the Garden House Hotel at Cambridge in September.

It was one of the happiest years of my life, and a wonderful time for us all—though Jack could enjoy only a part of it, and Tony, I fear, has forgotten virtually all of it. There can be, I should think, no more beautiful place in the world than the Cambridge of those days, the old college buildings, with their "backs," lush with grass and flowers as they can grow only in England, ranged along the slow-moving Cam. Our own hotel, with its lawn and gardens, also "backed" to the river. I was honored by being made a member of Downing College and had at least one dinner each week with the Fellows at the college. But my—and the family's—acquaintanceship extended far beyond Downing. Our best friends, if I may venture to make any comparisons among the many who were so amazingly hospitable and generous, were perhaps Sir Lionel Whitby, the Master at Downing and at the time also vice-chancellor of the university, and his wife Lady Whitby, George Woods of Downing, C. F. D. Moule of Clare College, the C. H. Dodds (Jesus College), the John A. T. Robinsons (Clare), and the Henry Chadwicks (Queens). With all of these friends we kept contact after our Cambridge year and with all of them, except Sir Lionel, George Woods and Professor and Mrs. Dodd (who have died) we have remained in touch.

The other later leaves from Union were for a semester only. One, in 1961, was spent in Claremont, California, where Pomp Colwell, then president of the Claremont School of Theology, offered me the opportunity of teaching a course for the semester and generously made provision for our comfort. Only Lois and I went this time. Tony was in school in New York, and Lois's parents were good enough to forsake for six months their home in Atlanta in order to stand *in loco parentis*. Jack, having completed his college degree with great distinction, a four-year tour of duty in the navy, and his Ph.D. degree in philosophy at Yale, was now teaching at C. W. Post College on Long Island. The last Union sabbatical, in 1965, I shall speak of more appropriately in another connection.

I have referred to a certain maturation which took place during my Union Seminary years and, given the limits of this sketch, it remains only to indicate a little more fully what it involved. I use the word *maturation* without, I hope, too much presumption, because I am not meaning to make an objective assessment as to either the truth of the intellectual judgments I found myself making or the rightness of the actions I found myself taking. Rather, I have in mind only the fact that both judgments and actions represented, it seems to me in retrospect, ends toward which my experience had all along been pointing.

Some of these "ends"—my mature opinions on several matters—have been anticipated in this narrative; and I cannot, in any case, attempt anything like a full account of how my thought has changed over the years on every subject that has concerned me or where it had arrived when my time at Union ended with my retirement in 1966 (as if on most subjects it had "arrived" at all, or has yet!). But one very general tendency in my thinking I must speak of here, a tendency present, I believe, since my first Chicago experience, but clarified for me and confirmed during my Union years and leading me to a theological position which can claim perhaps some measure of coherence and can be defended with some assurance. At any rate, *I* can defend it so. I mean the tendency to find the source of authority, the norm, of Christianity—indeed, the very meaning of the name—in the Church.

By "the Church" in such a statement, I mean, not something institutional (although it is hard to believe it could have survived, or can survive, without some institutional structure), but a definite, identifiable, historically created *community.* Now the word *community* is primarily, not a quantitative, but a qualitative term; that is, it designates primarily, not a collection of people, but a kind of relationship among them. They are conscious participants in a common corporate existence of some kind, be it family, nation, or what not. They are conscious sharers in the possession, or experience, of something precious, peculiar to themselves. The Greek word *koinonia,* which can be rendered in English as "communion," or "partnership," or "sharing," or "fellowship," is never in the New Testament to be translated as "community," in the sense in which we ordinarily use that term. That sense represents an enlargement of the Greek term, so as to make it mean, not the "fellowship" or "sharing" itself, but a group of persons among whom presumably a "fellowship" or "sharing" exists. Often when we use the word *community* the emphasis falls more upon the fact that a number of persons are involved than upon the shared experience which binds them together. But when we speak of the Church as "a historical community," if we are being at all true to the New Testament meaning of the term, we are thinking primarily of the precious common experience, shared in by millions over many generations, which makes it the particular community it is.

And what is this "precious common experience"? It consists in a common memory of, and loyalty to, Jesus as the true and loving person he was and in a common experiencing of the Spirit as being both the Presence of God and the continuing Presence of this same person—the two "Presences" being, *in experience,* inseparable and all but identical. This, it seems to me, is not a theoretical definition, or the statement of a norm, but is simply a description of what the Christian finds true about himself and has found true ever since the Resurrection (which was itself an inference from the experience of this "continuing Presence"). The essential, overarching, and to the Christian indubitable, miracle of Christianity, what we speak of as "the act of God in Christ," was God's bringing into being around Jesus of this shared existence, the making possible through him of this shared experience. All the traditional beliefs about the unique "nature" of Jesus, about his "divinity" as different *in kind* from the divinity in every man—beliefs which have been so unnecessarily divisive among Christians and between Christians and Jews—all such beliefs represent our fumbling efforts to explain a unique *event*, which was the creation around Jesus of a new community. And the explanation of the uniquely divine meaning of this event and this community lies, not in history at all, even in the man Jesus, but in Him who transcends history but is ultimately sovereign over it and exercises His activity within it. This is "God as known in Christ."

I have never said, though some have understood me so, that it is *only* through Christ—that is, *only* in the community created around Jesus, remembered and still known—that God is known. Indeed, I have often affirmed that if this were true He could not be God. For in Him, by definition, "all things live and move and have their being" and He is "the light that lighteth every man that cometh into the world." But I have recognized what it seems to me is obviously and necessarily true, that God is known *in a distinctive way* through the historical event of Christ and in the community in which that event has been perpetuated; and I have made some effort to describe that distinctive way.

Earlier in this account I have spoken of the evangelical piety in which I was nurtured and of how the life of our little family was lived almost completely within the church. We should have repudiated the word "Catholic," except in the much diluted sense in which we thought of it in saying

the Apostles' Creed. But by the time I reached Union I had
come to see that my father was a Catholic, however far he
may have been from thinking of himself as such. He and the
community he and we belonged to stood in a historical succession and shared in a historical communal existence. We
thought at the time that we had other sources of authority
and assurance than this shared existence—namely, the Bible
and the Spirit as separate from the Church—but in thus
thinking, I now saw, we had been mistaken. We had been
mistaken, not simply in opinions about things important to
us, but mistaken in that deeper, more significant way: we
were misunderstanding and misinterpreting ourselves. The
basic fact about us as Christians was our sharing in the historical Church's life; only in virtue of that fact did we know
the meaning of either Bible or Spirit. Moreover, the depth of
our sharing was the measure of our knowing. For the Bible
was the product and expression of the community's life, and
the Spirit, in the distinctively Christian sense of that term,
was the animating principle of its existence.

I told much earlier in this narrative of the struggle I had
as a boy when I was first confronted with the idea that the
Bible was not, as it were, divinely dictated, and therefore
magically infallible, but was throughout a human book, a
record of human experience: the experience of the Christian
community at its inception and of the ancient Hebrew community with whose history its own history was inseparably
continuous. I felt compelled to say then, "If we have only the
Church, we have nothing." But slowly over many years I had
come to see that in having the Church, in the full qualitative
sense in which I have been using the term, we have everything: God, Spirit, atonement or reconciliation, love, joy
peace, and hope—the whole experiential meaning of
"Christ," whether in creed or prayer.

But this is not the place to set forth the meaning and implications of a theological position. How could I think of

doing here what a number of books have tried to do with only
fair success? My present intention has been to refer to it as
the point to which, even from my youth, my efforts to make
sense of what was given me in my experience as a Christian
had been leading.

I have just said that my books of a theological kind
have been only fairly successful in winning assent or approval
from my colleagues, and I suspect that no more than this
could be said of the effects of my teaching among my
students. I do not suppose that any teacher or writer on
such matters as my books have dealt with—not only the
theologically oriented ones but the earlier ones as well—is
ever entirely pleased with the responses he evokes. He will
always feel that what he has said or written should have
more attention and wider acceptance than it actually re-
ceives, or deserves. I should think this was probably true of
the great theological writers of my generation—of such men
as the Niebuhrs, or Tillich, or Barth, or Bultmann—although
so enormous has been their influence that they may not
have felt the kind of disappointment likely to be felt by
the lesser man, the less widely and seriously listened to,
who nevertheless is persuaded that he too has something
important to say. This disappointment, needless to say, cannot be separated from the sinful pride which corrupts us
all, but it does not need to be explained entirely in this
way.

I believed, and still believe, that in my short book on
Paul's letter to Philemon I made a true and important contribution to our knowledge, not only of that letter, but also
of the origins of the New Testament canon. My disappointment that my hypothesis has been so generally ignored or
so quickly dismissed is not simply hurt pride. The same thing

can be said about my book on Marcion, although here I
recognize that I have presented a more vulnerable case.
I have had greater satisfaction in the reception given to a
suggestion about the chronology of Paul's career made in
two articles published in 1936 and 1939 and later embodied
in my book *Chapters in a Life of Paul.*

But most of my books have been concerned with christology (the meaning of Christ), or with some aspect of it—
*The Man Christ Jesus, Christ the Lord, On the Meaning of
Christ, The Death of Christ, The Church and the Reality of
Christ, Myth and Truth, The Humanity and Divinity
of Christ,* and a few others. Although none of these books has
come anywhere near to being a best seller, I cannot but hope
that together they have been successful, not only in making
my theological position known to more than a few, but also
in helping some of these readers to arrive at a more satisfying
theological position of their own. I am under no illusion
that they are great books, but I believe they mark out a
distinctive path and that the path is in the right direction.
Of all my books, none of them large, I am not sure but that
I think the most important, at any rate the one in which I
have most satisfaction, is among the smallest and least pre-
tentious of them. *Life in Christ Jesus* is a book which is less
concerned with theology than with Christian experience itself. But however all of this may be—and I am obviously
not the one to judge—my books and what I have given
to my students are my life's work; and I have some trust
that, after casting away the dross, God will find something
there to "build into" that "holy temple" of which the writer
to the Ephesians speaks, that "dwelling place of God in the
Spirit."

But if I must confess—as I have—to occasional hurts to my
pride, I must confess also to many more gratifications of it
than I have deserved. I have spoken of opportunities to give
lectures on distinguished foundations—at Yale, Harvard,

Chicago, Oberlin, Duke, University of Virginia, and many others. Honorary degrees have come, not only from my own college and seminary, but also from the Philadelphia, Berkeley, and General seminaries, and from Glasgow University. I was honored by terms as president of both the Society of Biblical Literature and the American Theological Society. The faculty and trustees of the Divinity School at the University of Chicago at one time were generous enough to make me "the alumnus of the year," and I treasure the plaque they gave me.

But chief among such honors and the one in which I must always find greatest satisfaction is the volume in recognition of my work with which I was presented in 1967— *Christian History and Interpretation,* edited by William R. Farmer of Southern Methodist University and Richard R. Niebuhr of Harvard, both former students of mine, and by C. F. D. Moule, the Lady Margaret's Professor at Cambridge and as dear a friend as I have. This handsome book of 460 pages, published by the Cambridge University Press, contains essays by eighteen of my former students and other colleagues and friends, not to speak of the comprehensive bibliography of my writings compiled by John Hurd and a most kindly assessment by John Bennett of my work at Union. I had never dreamed of even the possibility of such a gift as this! Would it be possible not to take pride in it? I tried to thank my friends for it, but how could I succeed? This generous concerted action by so many distinguished men atones many times over for the petty disappointments in which I had sometimes allowed myself selfishly to indulge.

During all my life thus far I had been a member of the Methodist Church. In 1919, as I have told, I was "admitted on trial" as a minister. In 1924 I was ordained a deacon, and in 1926 an elder. I was "appointed" by Bishops Candler or Denney to my several brief pastorates in the old Baltimore Conference of the Southern Methodist Church and to the Emory University teaching post of which I have spoken. In 1929, however, when I decided to accept the invitation to Fisk University, Bishop Denney, who happened to be the presiding bishop that year, refused to appoint me there. Since I was determined to go, I was consequently and perforce "located"—that is, separated from active membership in the conference, though not from the church; nor was I deprived of my status or office as an ordained minister. Since never again was I to be employed under Methodist auspices, my connection with that denomination tended to become more and more a merely formal link, although nothing could have broken, or ever can or will, the living bond between me and the remembered community in which I was nurtured and largely formed.

As early as 1932, while I was at Fisk, I felt myself drawn to the Episcopal Church and had, around that time, a number of what might be called counseling sessions with Dr. C. P. Wilmer of St. Luke's Church in Atlanta, about the possibility of my entering its ministry. Because I am by nature a conservative, and besides was emotionally deeply attached to the denomination to which my father had belonged, I shrank from the change. And yet I wanted a more active and wholehearted relation with the institutional church than I then had, and no other church than the Episcopal appealed to me at all. I believe that I should then have taken the radical step of seeking confirmation and ordination in that church if I had not been repelled by a conversation, arranged for me by Dr. Wilmer, with the Bishop of Atlanta, who was as formidable and forbidding as Dr. Wilmer had been receptive and sympathetic. It was perhaps just as well that it was so, for had I been really ready on the basis of

firm conviction to enter the Episcopal Church, the attitude of this bishop, or of any other, would not have deterred me. The inclination, however, despite this discouragement, remained. I have hinted of its existence in speaking of my inability to accept the invitation to the Drew Theological Seminary in 1948–49. But it was not till 1956 that I felt enough conviction to make a decisive move.

This conviction was based on the growing sense of the importance of the Church, of which I have spoken, and which, it seemed to me, came nearer to being authentically acknowledged in Anglicanism than in any other church. I decided that I wanted to become an Anglican, and yet I was unwilling even to appear to deny the validity of the ministry I had been called and ordained to in the Methodist Church. I began to consider whether it might be possible for me to be confirmed in the Episcopal Church without its requiring the renunciation of my membership and ministerial office in the church of my father and my youth.

My first decisive action was to discuss this possibility with a dear friend, Theodore O. Wedel, who was a canon of the Cathedral in Washington and Warden of the College of Preachers there. He promised to make inquiries. A little later he wrote me that the "experts" in canon law whom he had consulted were of the opinion that a minister in another church could not be confirmed in the Episcopal Church without having first renounced his former ministry. He himself was obviously not convinced that this was true and suggested that I consult with James Pike, who was then the Dean of the Cathedral of St. John the Divine in New York, a neighbor and friend—indeed, a former student of mine. Jim Pike's reply, while not discouraging, was also somewhat ambiguous and uncertain as to whether what I wished was possible. Foreseeing possible complications and embarrassments and at the same time not having any strong sense of urgency, I let the matter rest.

A year or so later, however, a very surprising happening brought the issue to a head. The president of the Episcopal students' organization at Union, a body of about eighty members, informed me that the group wanted me to accept the relationship of faculty advisor. I cannot express either my surprise or my joy in this invitation. I had known that the Episcopal students had an organization and that weekly celebrations of the Eucharist were held in the smaller of Union's two chapels. But I had not attended even one of these services or had any contact whatever with the organization. Nor did any student, or for that matter any member of the faculty, know of the conversations and correspondence I had had with Jim Pike and Ted Wedel. I asked David Edman, the spokesman of the group who called on me, whether he and his associates had taken sufficiently into account the anomalousness of a non-Episcopalian faculty adviser. Was it possible that they might be embarrassed in their relations with the Episcopal Church? He did not think so; but I asked him to consult further with others and to make quite sure the group wanted me to serve, telling him that while I would treasure nothing in my life at Union more than the proposed relationship, nevertheless I, too, wanted to think of the matter for several days.

My hesitation grew partly out of the fear that my accepting the invitation might embarrass the student organization with Episcopalians outside the seminary—but not altogether out of this fear. I thought of my Episcopal colleagues on the faculty and of a possible feeling on their part—entirely natural and understandable—that the students should have looked to one of them. A conversation with a close friend among these, however, rather settled my misgivings on this score. This conversation, as I recall, was initiated by him on the basis of information he had received from the student group. He felt that it would be proper for me to hold the office. So when the students confirmed their invitation, I said that I was very gratefully ready to accept it.

I felt that this action of the students definitely settled the issue of church membership for me, and I moved with determination toward the end I had so often considered. I spoke to Norman Pittenger, a warm friend at the General Theological Seminary, renewing the question I had originally raised with Ted Wedel—whether I might be confirmed without any renunciations. He saw no reason for any but an affirmative answer and advised that I speak with John Krumm, who was then chaplain of Columbia University and who might be willing to admit me to his next confirmation class, a group, mostly students, whom he would be preparing for membership in the Episcopal Church. I did speak to John Krumm, who was not only positive in his own attitude but able to assure me later that Bishop Donegan of the Diocese of New York had been consulted and that he was graciously willing to approve of my being confirmed under the conditions I have described. I was given instruction in John's next class and was confirmed early in 1959. The officiating bishop was Bishop Boynton, the Suffragan. The Episcopal students at Union, with whom by this time I had become warmly and closely identified, were a large part of the congregation at the service in the Columbia Chapel.

Although it was taken late in my life, this was one of the most significant steps I have ever taken and one in which I have found the greatest possible satisfaction. I am deeply grateful to my several advisers, Ted Wedel, Jim Pike, Norman Pittenger, and John Krumm, and to Bishops Donegan and Boynton. But I am even more grateful to David Edman, Mary Hotchkiss, and the other Episcopal students at Union, who recognized me as belonging to them before I had fully realized the fact myself, whose generous action precipitated a move I had hesitated to make, and whose affection and loyalty supported me in it and in what followed from it.

I might add here that when I had to give up my position as faculty advisor in 1966, it was taken by my beloved friend, Ian Macquarrie, who had also became an Anglican partly under the influence of this same student group.

Lois could not see her way to being confirmed when I was, although, knowing my mind, she wanted to be. But two years later she was freely and gladly ready, and she and Tony were also confirmed—at the Church of St. John in Ashfield, Massachusetts, near our Rowe summer home, by Bishop Hatch of Western Massachusetts. Until this should happen—and it happened entirely on her and Tony's initiative—I had not felt that I wanted to seek ordination in the Episcopal Church. But once she and Tony had joined me, I did apply. After the necessary canonical examinations I was ordained deacon on May 19, 1962, by Bishop Donegan, and six months later, priest. My desire not to make any renunciations was respected still. The order of service, when I was made deacon, included this item:

> The Bishop of New York will state the Church's mind in the matter of this particular candidate:
>
> John Knox, who is already a minister of Christ, now desires to be made a deacon in this Church. He has satisfied the Ecclesiastical Authority in this Diocese that he accepts the doctrine, discipline and worship of this Church. We are about to confer upon him the grace and authority of Holy Orders as this Church has received them and requires them for the exercise of the ministry therein.

This entire statement meant, and means, much to me, but especially the clause, "who is already a minister of Christ."

As the time approached for my retirement from the faculty at Union in the late spring of 1966, Lois and I were guests at several farewell parties, most of them under gracious faculty auspices. But the occasion which will always have the warmest place in our memories is the surprise party arranged by the Episcopal students of the seminary. It *was* a surprise in fact—that is, to me; Lois had been let in on the secret. I thought I was going to a small dinner party. I found myself surrounded by more than a hundred friends, most of them students and their wives or husbands, but some from outside, including Bishop Donegan.

This expression of loyalty and love is my most happy single memory of Union.

Chapter 8

Our Life in Austin: 1965 - 1972

I RETIRED AT Union at the normal retirement age of 65, although if I had wanted to remain longer, I should have been permitted another three years. I chose to leave at the earlier time, not only because the burdens of my Union Seminary life were becoming too heavy and because New York City was obviously not the most suitable environment for one who had a heart ailment, but also because of a strong desire I had been feeling for several years to spend my last working years in a seminary of the Episcopal Church, in which I had finally come to rest. Since Lois and I shared in a wish to return, at least for a while, to the South, with which our earliest memories and oldest associations indissolubly bound us, we hoped that, if we were fortunate enough to be invited to an Episcopal seminary, it would be located in that region.

There were now only the two of us involved. Jack was still at C. W. Post College, but was soon afterward to become associate professor, and several years later professor, of philosophy at Drew University in Madison, New Jersey. He was married to a charming girl, Alida van Bronkhorst, and not long after their move to Madison, they were to give us two beautiful grandchildren, a boy, Trevor, and fifteen months later, a girl, Amethy. Tony, having finished his elementary and high school work in New York, was by this time in the midst of his college course at Emory in Georgia. Soon after completing it at Georgia State College, he was to gain his own lovely wife, Jean Bolinger who, like Alida, has become our beloved daughter.

As early as 1964 I let it be known to two friends in two southern Episcopal seminaries that in 1966 I should welcome an opportunity of short-term employment in one of them. One of these friends was R. Francis Johnson, a favorite student of mine at Union years before, who was then professor of Old Testament at the Episcopal Theological Seminary of the Southwest at Austin, Texas. Frank kindly spoke of the matter to his colleagues at that institution and to the dean, Dr. Gray Blandy. The consequence was the kind proposal that Lois and I spend at Austin the sabbatical semester which had been granted me for the spring of 1965. I would teach a class with meetings only once a week and would thus have time for the work I had already planned to do— which happened to be the translations I had promised to make for *The New American Bible*. Since it was understood among us that this arrangement, if it proved to be successful and satisfactory to us all, might lead to the later appointment I had wanted for the years 1966–69, we were especially happy to accept it.

I might say at once that it did prove itself well enough for this appointment to be made. Our first semester at Austin was followed, after the lapse of my single final year at Union, by a period of regular employment which, owing to several contingencies and the generosity of the faculty and board of the seminary, stretched itself from the expected three years to an actual six. So important, however, was the introductory semester in establishing our relations with faculty and students at Austin, and even with many alumni, that I shall make no attempt in this account to separate it from the longer period which followed. Our Austin life seems to have begun in 1965 and to have ended in 1972. Despite very serious illnesses for both of us—illnesses distressingly persistent in Lois's case and, in mine, causing occasional interruptions of my work and, toward the end, the substantial reduction of it—despite all this, both of us look back on these Austin years as being, in many ways, the happiest years of our lives.

Austin itself, the capital city of Texas, is a lovely city— without doubt one of the most attractive residential cities in our country. Its terrain, especially on the western side, is hilly, almost mountainous. Several lakes lie within the town or in its immediate vicinity and a number of beautiful parks. A few brooks are permitted to run through the city, and there is abundant green everywhere. Most residences are private houses; there are relatively few apartment buildings. The town has grown, less around industry and business, than around state and national government institutions and the University of Texas. Although it is far from ideal, there is a relatively just and amicable relationship among the ethnic components of the population. Parish church life was very much a part of the ethos of the place. We soon found a home in the St. David's parish, and its rector, Charles Sumners, and his wife Virginia, as well as many members of the parish, became almost at once very loyal and affectionate friends. We had never before been so pleasantly and congenially situated.

We went to the Episcopal Theological Seminary of the Southwest at a time of rapidly approaching crisis in its affairs. It had been established only fifteen years earlier with the help of several generous gifts and for some time before our arrival had been housed in its own attractive modern buildings, well designed for their several uses (library, administration, classrooms, dormitory). A beautiful chapel, which had been planned from the beginning but the building of which had for some reason been delayed, was erected in

1965–66. The campus was small and compact but quite lovely, with well-kept lawns and gardens and many old trees belonging to the several evergreen types indigenous to the semitropical region. On the board of trustees were represented most of the dioceses of the Episcopal Church in Texas and in adjoining states to the north and west of it.

The faculty, which during the first year or so of the institution's life had consisted of only three men, each giving only part of his time, had quickly become a strong one, adequate to the range of a theological curriculum and also to the growing number of students who, it is my impression, must at times have been as many as one hundred or more. The men and women in the faculty were competent and able, and more than a few were distinguished, or have become such, for their academic achievements. The library was excellent, for high priority had always been given to the maintaining and increasing of its strength, both in the acquiring of previously published books—many of them out of print— and in keeping abreast of new publication. In such a picture one would hardly see the makings of a crisis. Nevertheless a crisis was imminent when we went to Austin in 1965.

It is not for me to describe in any detail how the crisis had arisen or to analyze the elements which composed it, nor could I hope to do so with any adequacy. I had only just come, and anything I may now say about such matters rests on impressions I gradually acquired from occasional comments of others or on inferences I drew from the situation as I found it. The immediate and altogether obvious exigency was financial. The institution had for years been living by borrowing on the value of its grounds and buildings. But more important than this lack of funds, and largely explaining it, was an alienation of the institution from its constituency, the Episcopal Church of the area, and particularly the bishops of the several supporting dioceses. Equally important

and perhaps even more basic were strains within the institution itself—estrangements within the board, within the faculty, and between the board and the faculty.

All of these stresses were owing largely to the presence on
the faculty, until a year or so before our coming, of a dominant minority of strong men whose conception of the seminary's nature and function was widely regarded as entirely
unrealistic and indeed fundamentally false. I had not
known, and do not know, any of this minority—I do not
know even the names of some of them—and my picture of
them may be quite mistaken and unfair. But it is the picture
I received, and all I am professing to do is to present that
picture—a picture based on no inquiries of my own but on a
few hints from my colleagues, on a few more explicit statements by some students and alumni, on what I know from
quite other sources about some of these men and, most of all,
on my observation of the abysmally low morale I found in
the institution as a whole. I am sure the picture cannot be
altogether wrong.

The minority's conception of the seminary was that of a
graduate school of religion, not a place for the education of
ministers. They did everything possible, I gathered, to dissociate the institution from the church in any but the most
formal sense. No reader of what I have written will need to
be told that I am not unsympathetic with graduate schools
of religion, although I believe the best possible ones will always have some kind of confessional basis. The impression
which, rightly or wrongly, I got of the men of whom I am
speaking is that they not only denied the need for such a
basis but actually held few personal theological convictions
of a Christian kind themselves. But however that may be, if
anything was clear in Austin in the sixties, it was that the
potentiality of such an advanced and more or less secular
school of religion just did not exist there. The students, now
very few, were mostly men in their thirties or forties who had

turned from other careers (in all the cases I knew, successful ones) under the compulsion of a call to become priests of the church. Toward these men, except perhaps the most brilliant, the attitude of the dominant minority was, as far as I could gather, one almost of contempt, certainly one devoid of much sympathy or pastoral concern. Anyone's conviction that he was "called" into the priesthood was dismissed as "piety," which by definition was despicable. I could feel no surprise that the church in the area, upon which alone the institution had to depend for both moral and financial support, had drawn away.

I do not want to leave the impression that there were not members of the faculty who had been entirely out of sympathy with the attitudes of the men to whom I have been referring. Such an impression would be grossly untrue. I never joined a faculty so many of whose members were so obviously unhappy. Some of them at least had been torn between deep personal Christian conviction and a desire to share it, on the one hand, and, on the other, the strong and aggressively expressed opinion of an arrogant few that, even if deep personal Christian conviction was possible at all, the sharing of it in an academic setting was entirely inappropriate.

My own first intimation of the situation I have been describing goes back to the time of my first class. Lois and I had come in February of 1965 knowing nothing of the past history of the seminary or of the crisis in morale of which I have spoken. I was to teach a course in the christology of the New Testament, and twenty or twenty-five students, I should say, had enrolled for the class. I was quite amazed by the response made to my first lecture. I had never experienced anything like it in all my years of teaching. The lecture itself had certainly not been an extraordinary one, or by any standard a particularly good one. It was in substance the same lecture I had often given in opening a course on our theme, and it had never before been heard with more than ordinary interest. But this time it was received with an eagerness for which I was entirely unprepared and which I did not in the least degree understand. At the end of the two-hour session the students crowded around my desk to talk further—ostensibly, at least, about some of the points made in the lecture.

I soon discovered, however, that it was not the lecture itself which had so excited them—or, at any rate, the larger number of them. It was rather the fact that I had spoken in a manner which suggested that I believed what I was saying to be true and important and that I assumed it was also true and important to them—in a word, that we were discussing a shared and precious faith. Knowing my colleagues as I soon did, I could not, and cannot, believe that such an attitude toward the subject matter of theology and toward one's fellow students in it was not felt and exemplified by more than a few of them. But apparently the students for some reason had not expected it from me. Moreover, I could not but infer, they had not regarded it as characteristic of the institution as a whole in its teaching function.

I had opened the class session with a short prayer. This simple act seemed to have made an inordinate impression— not the prayer itself, of course, but the fact that it was offered. I had always opened my class meetings at Union with prayer, as in fact we were required by faculty bylaws to do. I suspect that this rule was beginning to be ignored by the time we left; but I never had any trouble keeping it. Even without the rule, I should have welcomed the opportunity, and should have regarded it as altogether appropriate, to pray with my class. Not that I should have felt so about *any* class! Indeed, I have always felt a strong aversion to prayer of a purely formal sort, or to the offering of prayer on public occasions, or on any occasion when it was not to be assumed that all the persons present were prepared to share in it. For this reason, in my college teaching, not only did I feel no inclination to open classes with prayer, but I should have refused to do so. But in a *seminary,* among persons committed to Christian faith and service, the situation was surely quite different. Why should we not pray together? How better could we lay the foundation and set the frame for discussing the vital matters we were concerned with? Common worship was the presumably acknowledged context of all our academic work.

The crisis which was imminent when we first visited Austin in 1965 fully came in 1967, just after we had come back for our longer stay. The trustees took the position that the institution should become what alone it could be, a seminary, or it would have to close its doors. This was no idle threat because the budget had been out of balance for so many years that with the spring of 1967 the institution's borrowing power had literally been exhausted. The raising of new funds was made conditional upon our taking a realistic view of our nature and function and reducing our expenses. These conditions were met—the latter through the departures of many of our staff for more congenial or more secure positions and by various economies. I might say at once that the necessary funds were raised, largely through the efforts of Bishop Richardson of the Diocese of Texas, who was the president of the board. The relations between the seminary and the church began to improve (and are still improving). Communication between the faculty and the board was opened and became ever freer and more friendly. The student body began to increase, and its morale was lifted, becoming indeed excellent. Dean Blandy decided to return to the pastorate in 1967, and after an interval of a year (during which Frank Johnson was acting dean) Hudnall Harvey succeeded him and proved to be an extraordinarily

wise and able leader. He was still in office when we left
Austin in May of 1972.

I said early in this part of my story that our six years in
Austin were very happy years for Lois and me, but I have
said very little to explain or support that statement. Indeed,
I have spoken largely of a crisis, which was anything but
agreeable. But this was rapidly approaching its end when we
arrived. Actually, despite the controversy and conflict in the
background, it was the serenity of the Austin period, as com-
pared with earlier terms of service, which helped make it the
happy period it was for both of us. For one thing, our life became simpler. Ill health or the threat of it forced us to stay
at home. I could, with good conscience, decline all invitations to lecture or preach, not only in distant places, but also
in Austin itself. The same limitations of health and strength
prevented my undertaking any serious research. I could devote such energies as I had simply and only to my work with
students.

This work was itself unexacting and entirely congenial.
We had few if any graduate or advanced students in New
Testament. My courses were elementary, beginning courses,
or else electives dealing with matters with which I was already fairly familiar. I must confess that during these years I
did very little study of the hard sort and made no effort to
keep up, except in a most cursory fashion, with what was
going on in my field. My lectures, if they should be dignified
by such a name, came out of such knowledge as I had already accumulated, such judgments as I had already
formed. They represented my own response, often quite
spontaneous, to the biblical materials we were considering. I
knew that this was my last stint of teaching, and I allowed
myself to do what I had always wanted to do—namely, to

talk with my students about the *meaning* of Scripture (especially Paul), what its writers were trying to say to their readers and what they might still be saying to us. For discussions of most technical literary and historical questions I referred them to books and articles. My classes were small, and there was ample opportunity for the exchange of experience and opinion—a sharing which meant much to me and, I believe, to my fellow students also.

The faculty was small and of distinguished quality: Lawrence Brown, Frank Doremus, Arnold Hearn, Nelle Bellamy, William Green, Harold Booher, Frank Sugeno, and Richard Woods, not to mention the several who left the faculty not long after our coming. I have already referred to Gray Blandy, Frank Johnson, and Hudnall Harvey. Several members of the administrative staff were equally important to us. There were opportunity and sufficient leisure for closer acquaintance and more frequent intercourse with my colleagues and their wives than either Lois or I had ever enjoyed before, and the lives of us both were greatly enriched by the close friendships we made and hope ever to keep alive.

Living within a block of us were Charles and Dorothy Hartshorne, with whom I had been somewhat acquainted as long ago as my time on the faculty at Chicago, where he was then a brilliant young member of the department of philosophy. He was now professor of philosophy at the University of Texas, had become the most able and distinguished interpreter and developer of Whitehead's thought in the world, and as such was of as much interest and importance to theologians as to philosophers. Both Lois and I were warmly grateful for the opportunities we had of renewed and closer friendship with both him and his wife; and it was a great privilege to join others in our faculty in bringing him at least a little more into the seminary's life and in making his vastly significant contribution to theology better known there, and more available.

Also greatly rewarding to us were the warm relationships we had with some of the church leaders of the region, notably with Bishop Everett Jones of San Antonio and Bishop Richardson of Houston. I have spoken already of Charles and Virginia Sumners. Especially in view of the distance between Austin and Houston, Bishop Richardson was extraordinarily solicitous, calling on us in our various illnesses, assisting us in many ways in times of stress. I shall always remember with particular gratitude his kindness and that of his wife, Gene, in insisting that I be a guest in their home when Lois was spending some weeks at St. Luke's Hospital in Houston. The same kind of hospitality was several times extended to us by Thomas Sumners, the rector of the Church of St. John the Divine in Houston, and his wife Doris.

But it was chiefly the relationships we came to have with many students and their families which made our Austin life so extraordinarily stimulating and happy. In so small and compact a community there were many opportunities for companionship. Needless to say, it was in my classes and in work connected with them that I could come best to know my students, and they me. They were soon joined in class by many of their wives; and other young people from the city began to attend as "auditors." In the final semesters there were as many of these as of the more regular members. With these visitors Lois and I soon became as well acquainted as with the seminary personnel itself, and we continue in close, affectionate contact with many of them.

Most of these townspeople, as well as not a few of the students—all devout and loyal churchmen of several denominations—were much concerned for the renewal of the institutional church's life. They felt this concern because they were finding a deep need of their own to which the institutional church was not adequately answering. This need was for an experiential ground for assurance of the meaning of their lives, of the meaning of human life—in a word, the need for God. They were groping for this fulfillment and in doing so were finding many others engaged, often almost desperately, in this same search.

These lay Christians, only the barest few of whom I knew in my classes, were forming, I quickly learned, in every part of Austin groups for prayer and study, for the confession of personal needs and the discussion of personal problems, for mutual sympathy and the sharing of experience. There were many groups of husbands and wives, but most of these gatherings were of either men or women—the women meeting in various homes at some convenient hour during the week, and the men very early in the morning before the day's work would have begun. I never attended one of these prayer groups, but I received many hints of what went on in them. One's first impression from my description may well be of the "Oxford Groups" of a few decades ago. I had reacted vigorously against these; but I knew only sympathy with this movement in Austin. It was not exhibitionist. It was neither fundamentalistic nor socially reactionary. Its members—if one can use that term when the movement was so unorganized and unselfconscious—although often theologically naïve, were eager to learn the truth about God and about themselves, about history, and about the present world and its needs. I found in it something of the vitality of primitive Christianity with its house churches, and of the early Wesleyan movement in England with its class meetings.

In such association as I had with many of the local leaders in this quiet movement of the Spirit I found myself back within the spiritual atmosphere in which I was reared and had the feeling that I had come full circle. Many of the participants I came, and Lois with me, to love with deep loyalty and affection. To not a few, especially Carolyn and Charles Huffman (if I may venture to mention two out of a very large class), both of us owe a great enrichment of our faith and life as Christians.

I shall mention only one other by name, Keith Miller. I soon learned through him that this lay group movement was not only characteristic of Austin but was of national scope. Persons—many of them hitherto in no relation with the organized churches—were everywhere being drawn together, indirectly at least under church auspices, by a realization of deep spiritual needs which secular society was not helping them to fulfill. Keith was himself a layman, with past experience in business, with considerable training in psychology and in the theological disciplines, and with quite extraordinary gifts as a communicator with the plain man. A person of high intelligence, discerning and honest about himself, and utterly without pretense or cant, both open and discriminating, with a realistic understanding of the human situation in our times as regards individuals and social structures, sensitive to what was essential in the Christian message and dedicated to making it relevant and available— he was rapidly becoming a spokesman for and to the growing national movement. He was—and of course still is— in constant demand as a speaker, and his books have sold, literally, in the hundreds of thousands, if not in the millions. His influence in Austin itself was enormous. I believed in him. And I have great hopes of the grass-roots movement to which he owes so much and which owes so much to him. I was deeply moved by the fact that participants in it (I suspect to their surprise) found in me, a theological professor thoroughly committed to the critical historical method in biblical study, a kindred spirit and came to think of me as one of themselves.

I have indicated that my work in Austin was virtually limited to Austin itself and indeed to the seminary. Not only did I accept no speaking engagements outside the city, and very few even within it, but I discovered I lacked the energy to do much intensive work of any sort. My writing in the early mornings consisted almost entirely in letters. I did attempt a little writing of a more sustained kind, however, and of it and the concerns out of which it grew I must briefly speak.

I have said enough in the course of this narrative to make clear that one of my firmest and most intimate convictions is that there can be no divorce between theology and devotion, that one cannot as a theologian write or speak truly about God if one has no experience of God, no "feel" of his reality and presence. As a philosopher, one may do so, but not as a theologian. And to claim that only a philosopher can speak truly about God would be as absurd as it would be to claim that no one can speak truly about music except a mathematician. I have heard professors of Bible speak almost as if they despised the Bible as having anything important or relevant or moving to say, or as having intrinsic value of any kind—indeed, as if they thought that only by despising it thus, or appearing to, could they teach it at all with any objectivity and therefore truth. A stranger, more monstrous, anomaly could hardly be conceived. Imagine its being made a necessary qualification of a teacher of Shakespeare that he should not be a lover of Shakespeare, or else be able to hide his love, or of a teacher of the classics that he should be, and certainly must appear to be, quite unmoved by the hexameters of Homer or Virgil! Who indeed but a lover of Homer can know Homer at all; and what can be the principal purpose of his teaching, if he have any purpose worth mentioning, except to bring his pupils to see and love what he sees and loves? And how can he hope to do this if he must carefully conceal that he sees and loves anything at all—if in fact he does!

I recall during my student days at Chicago hearing Professor Huth of the department of history say, as an aside, during a lecture on ancient Roman history, that it seemed significant to him, and also somewhat ominous, that at that time the greatest pieces of historiography in this country were being written by persons who were not professional historians. I recall his mentioning Sandburg's *Lincoln* and I believe he referred also to Freeman's *Robert E. Lee.* There were other references I did not recognize and do not remember. He accounted for this phenomenon by observing that professional historians had become so thoroughly limited and, it might almost be said, corrupted, by concern for "objectivity" that they were afraid to trust their own imaginative insights, not to speak of their own humanity, and that therefore, insofar as this was true, they were unable to get "on the inside" of either persons or events of the past.

But if so much as this can be said in disparagement of an attitude and method as applied to subjects in general, at any rate in the humanities, what can be said in its defense when one is dealing with one's own existence and the existence of one's hearers or readers and especially if the existence is really a corporate historical existence in which one's own and theirs is largely a sharing? But my early experience at Austin forced me to recognize on the basis of what I gathered to have been true earlier, that there were persons in positions of teaching responsibility in the church who either did not share in this existence, or were diligent in avoiding giving any impression that they did, and who gave no evidence, and made no pretensions, of sharing in the theological beliefs whose truth is implicit in this existence. I had also been forced to recognize the immense, the immeasurable, harm such teachers could do.

Since this situation was surely not unique, it is not surprising that there should have been widespread perplexity and distress among Christian believers generally, and that in more sophisticated circles the issue was being raised as to whether there was a Christian orthodoxy, and if so, how it could be defined. Could we any longer speak of "heresy," and if so, how was it to be identified and dealt with?

Associated with this issue, and for many even more troublesome, was the question of what responsibility the church had for the solution of large-scale economic, political, and racial problems, and how this responsibility could appropriately be exercised. These two sets of issues, not logically connected, were associated for many by what might be regarded as the accidental circumstance that many teachers and pastors who had lost faith in God had found a kind of compensation in a secularized version of the social gospel.

This "gospel" had originally been the expression of the church's sense of its mission, under the Father of all men, not merely to give the cup of water to the thirsty individual and to bind up his wounds, but also to challenge and change those unjust and inhumane structures of society which produce such needy individuals—and in such appalling numbers! Nothing could have been more true, or more appropriate to the church's nature, than the work of the saintly Walter Rauschenbusch near the beginning of the century in summoning the church to see and accept this mission. For him and for those who followed in his train—men like John R. Mott and Sherwood Eddy, as well as more critical and realistic disciples like Charles Morrison, Reinhold Niebuhr, John Bennett and a host of others—for all of these, concern about the social order was connected pervasively and inseparably with Christian devotion. Love for neighbor was an expression of the love of God. Christian social action, in virtue of that fact, had its own distinctive motivation and its own distinctive quality. But now, it appeared, for many who were traditionally and professedly Christian, perhaps even teachers of the church, the phrase "the love of God" had lost any vital meaning or any real truth, whereas "love thy neighbor" was very much alive. This led, not to an overemphasis upon the need for human compassion and social justice (as though that need could ever be overemphasized!), but rather to a divorcing of this social message from its original context, with the consequence of an enormous impoverishment of its content and the loss of its native religious quality and tone.

Against this distortion of the preaching of the social gospel there was widespread protest. Needless to say, there had always been many who objected to this gospel *per se*—that is, who resisted any attempt in either the teaching or the practice of the church to apply the Christian concern for justice and humanity to those established structures of society which denied both. Obviously, to satisfy such people, the sensitive and intelligent minister would have needed to deny his own soul—which he often did, and does! But to the ignorant and callous protests of this great number of professing Christians had now been added the voices of many more authentic Christians, who objected, not to an emphasis upon the church's responsibility in the social, economic and political realms, but to the essentially secular nature of that emphasis.

I recall a conversation, as early as the period of our residence in Nashville, with a professor at Vanderbilt—a conversation in which he was explaining why his parish, made up largely of university people, had recently been seeking the resignation of its pastor, a long-time friend of mine. It was not, he said, because the minister believed in racial equality and industrial democracy, and proclaimed his beliefs without fear or compromise, but rather because this was *all* he believed, or at any rate, all he proclaimed. "Indeed," he said, "we—almost all of us liberal and fairly enlightened citizens—fully agree with him and feel the reality of social injustice and the shamefulness of it as deeply as he does. The cause of our dissatisfaction is rather that he can do no more for us than to denounce these evils. We come to church to be fed and we find no food."

It is not surprising that thousands of laymen less enlightened than my Vanderbilt professor acquaintance should under such circumstances as these come to associate all social liberalism with a lack of concern for the devotional life and for the theological beliefs which are inescapably implied by it, and to suspect any effort of the church to promote social change as covering a lack of care for the individual's deep personal need of God, not to speak of a lack of capacity to serve this need.

The division, at any rate in the Episcopal Church, on the question of whether there was a Christian orthodoxy and therefore what should be called and dealt with as heresy, and the question of what was the church's responsibility for the social order—this division became, or threatened to become, so serious that the presiding bishop in 1967 appointed a commission to consider these questions and to advise him and the church as a whole as to how they should be answered. The commission, of which Bishop Bayne was chairman, invited ten persons or so to write letters of five thousand words, setting forth their views on the several issues. My own letter was published along with those of the others as a supplement to the report the commission soon afterward made.

I shall not try to give any adequate account of the content of my letter. It can be read in *Theological Freedom and Social Responsibility,* edited by Bishop Bayne. As for the church's responsibility for the social order, I hope I do not need to say I vigorously affirmed it, urging, however, that it be proclaimed and in practice discharged within an authentically Christian (as contrasted with a merely secular) context. As to the questions about orthodoxy and heresy, the point I emphasized was that the church is a distinctive culture, that it involves a distinctive way of life, and therefore inevitably some distinctive *beliefs,* or *ways of thinking,* about life's meaning; that the significant question is, not "What do I have to believe to be a Christian?"—such a question would always have seemed to me to be inappropriate—but rather, "What does a Christian inevitably find himself believing?" For "being a Christian" is, unquestionably, not primarily *believing* something, but rather is *being* something. It is sharing in a historical community's existence, belonging to the church understood as the community of the memory and Spirit of Christ, sensing its distinctive quality, loving it for what it is deeply felt to be—a total responding to what is given in it. All of this goes far beyond, and is definitely other than, accepting dogmatically stated "necessary beliefs." But although "being a Christian" is this and only this, nevertheless in this experience some positive beliefs are clearly implied and certain denials and doubts, certain kinds and degrees of unbelief, are just as clearly excluded. A Christian, for example, could hardly find himself denying the reality, and therefore the grace, of God, as some spokesmen for the church were doing.

Having been led to think of this "crisis of faith" within the church, I could not but continue to do so. When I was invited to give the Page Lecture at the Berkeley Divinity School in New Haven in early 1968, I took this theme as my topic; and my lecture later extended itself into a small book, *Limits of Unbelief*. In it I wrote, not for scholars, but for troubled Christians. More particularly I wrote for some of our students and their wives, among whom I had come to feel more poignantly than ever before both the rich spiritual reality of our fellowship in Christ and the urgent need of greater clarity and precision and firmness in our beliefs about it. Only by opening ourselves to our fullest capacity to the grace of God (and how can most of us Western men know this grace, whether we recognize this fact or not, apart from Christ?), and by seeing as truly and clearly as possible what this experience of grace necessarily implies about the nature of the world and of our life within it—only so, I urged, can any of us resist the pressures of that secularism which is steadily eroding the most precious values in our cultural heritage and threatening our very souls.

After my seventieth birthday had passed, I recognized that the time had come for me to give up active professional work entirely. I am under the impression that the rules of the seminary would have required that I do so in any case. But this question did not need to be raised. The state of Lois's health and mine dictated the decision. Despite the shortness of my tenure, the faculty and trustees were good enough to make me professor emeritus, as I am in Union's faculty. I find equal joy in both continuing relationships. We left Austin and Texas in May of 1972, feeling that we were leaving half our hearts behind us. Not only were we saying good-bye to many of our warmest and dearest friends, but we were also laying down the work to which we had been so long devoted and which had made up so large a part of the life of both of us.

We are learning, however, that there are compensations in leisure, especially when it is shared by two persons, each more than ever loving and beloved. There is opportunity for more constant mutual companionship and for more frequent intercourse with our children and grandchildren. There is time for rest, for reading, for music, for reflection, for prayer; time for such new friendships as one can make and for the cultivation, and sometimes the renewal, of old friendships as well; time for the giving of thanks and for the remembering of all one has reason to give thanks for. When, missing my work and my students, I am tempted to despondency, I find comfort in Milton's sonnet on his blindness, especially the words: "Who best bear his mild yoke, they serve him best" and "They also serve who only stand

and wait." But Milton, to his surprise, discovered that he could do more than this; and so perhaps shall we!

Nor are students altogether lacking. Old ones sometimes find us in our present retreat, gladdening our eyes and our hearts. More often they write us. Most of the letters come from former students (at Fisk, Chicago, Hartford, Union, or Austin) with whom relations, freed from all bonds of academic decorum, have developed through a continuing correspondence into equal and affectionate friendships. But occasionally an unexpected letter comes from a student, perhaps of long ago, who in a moment of impulsive kindness has written to thank me for some service I scarcely remember. I hardly need to say that such a letter brightens, not only the day, but also the prospect of all the days ahead. More rarely still I am surprised with a letter telling me that I was of help to some student in ways, or to an extent, of which I was entirely unaware.

I was speaking at some point in this narrative of rewards my career as an educator has brought: a few degrees, a few presidencies of societies, and the like. I should have referred to such things, not as "rewards" as if they were earned, but as "gifts" generously bestowed, as in truth they were. But if so much can be said about these external and transiently significant distinctions, what can one say about such a letter as this: ". . . It meant more than you can possibly know for me to be in your classes. You were with me through what must have been the darkest hours of my life. If God had not spoken to me through you, I could never have survived . . . I am forever grateful."

What, I ask again, can one say about such a letter? Is it pride which accounts for the joy such confessions from the hearts of friends—and we all sometimes receive them—bring to our own hearts? I am sure it is not so. On the contrary, these confessions strike at the very roots of our pride by setting our small, self-centered lives in true perspective in the greatness and goodness of God, and thus reveal, at least for the moment, the emptiness of all our pretentions. But if for a moment they take away our pride, they do so only to replace it with a deeper, truer satisfaction. Perhaps in such moments we have a glimpse of Jesus' meaning when he spoke of "treasures in heaven." As for myself, I cannot forget the many hurts I must have given and the many opportunities of helpfulness I have missed. But even so, can life offer a teacher or priest—and it has been my inestimable privilege to be both—a happiness greater than such testimonies yield?

As I read through the brief and summary sketch I have now finished, I am impressed with how *very* brief and summary it is. I recognized and mentioned in the Foreword two omissions I anticipated from the beginning. But now I am forced to recognize a far more glaring, and possibly less readily excusable, lack. The story I have told has been virtually confined to the small circle of my own life and the persons, places and events most closely associated with it. Except for an occasional reference to a war, or to a contemporary economic or sociological situation, or to some new, or newly dominant, trend or development in our culture, I have said little to indicate my awareness of having lived through the most tumultuous period of human history thus far, a period of change—ideological, technological, political, cultural—worldwide in its scope and fraught with possibilities of good and evil for mankind of which in my boyhood I could not have dreamed. And I have made no effort whatever to narrate or interpret this portentously "strange, eventful history," of which my own story is so minute a part. But surely my awareness of it can be assumed; and in view of my own limitations, not to speak of the limits of this book, my failure to attempt any analysis, or even description, of it can be understood.

With reference to it, I shall simply say that as I face the future—and this must be true of most of us—I do so with no little foreboding. Science and technology, for all their beneficent gifts, have released mighty, potentially destructive, forces which, at the moment at least, seem beyond our power to control. We can hardly fail to ask ourselves whether human beings—such men as you and I—are capable of rising, or of being raised, to that level of intelligence, imagination, and disinterested concern which is required if our world is to survive. As Reinhold Niebuhr reminded us decades ago, if that question can be seriously asked about us as individuals, how much more difficult a confident affirmative answer becomes when we ask it about nations and states! But I do not despair. Our planet has seen the births and deaths of many civilizations, but it has seen rebirths and renewals as well. And who will be so rash as to deny the possibility that, through a worldwide awakening to the realities of the human situation, such a renewal may yet happen in our time? Are there not signs to give us hope?

But if the worst should come and we destroy ourselves, whether in swift stages or in some total fiery debacle—even so, God's being does not depend upon man's fate on this planet. We know that, either late or soon, eventually this fate is death, as surely as death is the earthly fate of every man. But our faith and hope in God are not confined within this "bourne of time and place." Not merely from generation to generation, but from everlasting, to everlasting, he is God; and in ways beyond our understanding and in worlds beyond our imagining he will fulfill the loving purpose of his creative work.